TEAMWORK
NOT
PAPERWORK

A practical guide to using
the Construction (Design and
Management) Regulations 2007
to deliver better projects

TONY & PAUL
PUTSMAN McARTHUR

Published by CTT Publications
4 Oakwell Drive
Leeds
LS8 4AE

www.cttechnologies.co.uk

First published 2012
Text and images ©
Tony Putsman and Paul McArthur

ISBN: 978-0-9572863-0-6

CONTENTS

ACKNOWLEDGEMENTS

We would like to thank the following who have given us help, support and advice in producing a better book than we could have delivered on our own:-

Alan Muddiman
Mike Battman
Mick Jordan
Kris Moodley
Alistair Gibb
Ian Fleming
Richard Norman
Richard Ash
Don Ward
Paul Wilkinson
Bob Pedley
Peter Drenon
David Jones
Richard Vertigan
Alex Bell
Keith Laws
Mark Hodgson
Sarah Martin
Matt Campbell
Cath Orange

INTRODUCTION

Why we wrote this book

Any construction professional will tell you that, however well we do in delivering a project, some aspects won't go to plan - there is always scope to do it better next time.

This book has been written for people who want to do it better. Whether you are a lifelong practitioner or recent entrant into the construction sector, you need to think differently if you are to improve on current performance. We want to help you to do just that – think differently and then act differently.

When we say 'better', we mean better for the client, better for the project team and better for the end user.

It may come as a surprise to think that CDM 2007 can be the key to driving improvement in the Construction sector but that is the belief that lies at the heart of this book. Anyone who fails to understand this is overlooking the potential the CDM Regulations offer for significant improvements in time, cost and quality performance, as well as reducing the shocking toll of accidents and health problems resulting from construction operations.

There are substantial improvements to be gained, for the Client, the Project team, and individual workers, if a more 'people-centred' approach is taken to project risk management, with less emphasis on paper and more emphasis on engaging all participants in developing sound working methods.

At its heart, that is what CDM is all about.

So what's this book about?

Since the Construction (Design & Management) Regulations 2007 (CDM 2007) came into force on 6th April 2007, a number of books have been written to expand on the guidance contained in the very practical Approved Code of Practice (ACOP). Whilst many contain useful information on what is required of project teams under the revised regulations and how they differ from the original regulations they are generally written from a 'technical' perspective.

That is, they concentrate on what the individual sections of the regulations require of the various duty holders. It can be very difficult, from reading these books to gain an appreciation of the management principles behind the legislation, or to discern how project teams should behave in order to achieve the levels of performance required by these regulations and associated legislation.

Perhaps the biggest criticism of these texts is that they are written from a dispassionate perspective that ignores the human consequences of management failure.

This guide addresses CDM from the 'people' perspective. It explains in non-technical language how CDM encourages the project team to develop itself **first**. Then, as a team, the members can design and construct a facility that is safe to build operate and maintain, and in doing so can deliver a successful project in terms of quality, cost and personal satisfaction – a project in which the whole team can take pride.

This is not a 'Health & Safety' book, – we believe that good health and safety is simply an intrinsic aspect of good management. However, through its pages we will aim to highlight the high degree of correlation between the legal obligations imposed by the CDM regulations and other legislation, and the principles embedded in best practice management philosophy.

Like the CDM Regulations, this guide is relevant to construction projects of all sizes and types. Likewise, the principles of management contained in the following pages apply whether you are an experienced construction professional, a serial client, or a new entrant to the world of Construction.

Our hope is that this book will aid your understanding of why many projects fail to achieve their goals.

It will:

- Outline the steps which if initiated at the outset, can help teams like yours to achieve high quality, safe and economically efficient outcomes for your projects.
- Give you a thorough understanding of the CDM Regulations 2007
- Help you to understand why many projects fail to achieve their goals
- Show you how CDM can help you build the team – and thereby build better projects.

We hope to challenge you, inform you, and entertain you. We encourage you to adopt the principles in this book to help your teams achieve high-quality, safe, and economically efficient outcomes.

Enjoy!

Tony Putsman and Paul McArthur

SECTION 1

THE TROUBLE
WITH CONSTRUCTION

IN WHICH WE DISCOVER:

*What's going on in
construction*

*The origins of health
and safety law*

Why we need CDM

'Those who fail to learn the lessons
of history are condemned to repeat them.'

At its best, the UK Construction Industry can match the performance of its international competitors.

The successful completion of the facilities and infrastructure for the 2012 Olympics illustrates that in terms of design, construction performance and raising safety, health and environmental standards, it is possible to exceed expectations and attain a level of excellence of which any construction professional would be proud.

However, the Construction sector is a large and very diverse part of the UK economy where standards, both in terms of production and safety, can vary dramatically depending on the scale and nature of the work.

THE F – WORD

Let's begin by dividing construction projects into two categories:

Successful – where the project is completed on time, within budget, safely, and meets or exceeds client expectations

Unsuccessful – where time, cost, quality, safety or environmental performance falls significantly below what was hoped for when the client initiated the scheme.

Whilst being straightforward, this simple way of measuring success fails to take account of the wider picture. Ask different parties who have worked on the same project and you may get very different answers as to whether or not the project was 'successful'.

It's not really a surprise then that, anecdotally, it would appear that more projects fall into the second category than the first. Why is this - and what can we do to ensure success on our future projects?

At least part of the answer lies in the very nature of construction project teams. Imagine someone from outside of the Construction sector describing a construction project team. They might imagine the project team to be made up of people from a few different organizations working together - the client, an architect, the main contractor and his team. They might expect the contractor's team to include designers, steel erectors, bricklayers, electricians, and all the other trades and professions needed to complete the job.

Yet, as we know, the reality is quite different. In fact, these services are provided by many different organizations sub-contracted by the main contractor or the client.

Out of around 200,000 organisations working in the Construction sector in the UK, it has been estimated that over 90% employ <u>fewer than ten people</u>.

And of course, the organizations and individuals involved can be different from one project to the next. Imagine the 'outsider's' surprise when he discovers this:

"How on earth do you manage to communicate with each other?" he might ask.
"How do you manage to build the project without falling out?"
"How do you work together?"

The truth is that for many projects there isn't really a project *team* at all. In reality individuals get on and do their bit, and in many projects when it goes wrong they put their heads down and point at someone else.

And so the F-word we're thinking about is 'Fragmentation'. In many construction projects, the team is fragmented into small groups– each working largely on its own.

 THINK POINT:
Fragmentation of the team: - a failure to work as a coherent unit is at the heart of most failure in Construction.

FIG 1: TEAM RISK PROFILE FOR CONSTRUCTION PROJECTS

In reality, the 'Project Team' comprises a fluid combination of dedicated, long-term team members (particularly from the client organization and those of their key advisers) and transient, shorter-term members (e.g. suppliers, contractors, sub-contractors) who often make up the majority of the workforce. It is this group who will be most at risk of harm during the construction phase.

PROJECT MANAGEMENT OR RISK MANAGEMENT?

For other members of the team different concerns such as financial issues or the technical performance of the design will be more pressing issues. For these reasons, delivering a construction project, by its nature, is an exercise in risk management – where the risks and consequences associated with failure can be great.

Some failures are worse than others. Many projects exceed their budgets or suffer time over-runs. The Millennium Dome and Wembley Stadium are two high profile examples of projects that suffered major delays and/or cost over-runs but eventually outlived the problems associated with their construction and went on to achieve long term success.

Quality failures ranging from major defects to extensive snagging are often viewed as a normal part of project execution. The clutch failure on the London Eye and the initial baggage handling problems at Heathrow's new Terminal 5 underline the fact that otherwise successful projects can suffer from high profile quality (performance) failures.

So we can see that for a variety of reasons, every project presents its own unique circumstances:

1. The precise nature of the construction, combined with the composition of the project team, will differ to some degree, from project to project. Even where the facility itself is largely the same as on other sites, the location and ground conditions, proximity to other landowners' operations, interface with members of the public and other variables represent a combination of risks that is unique to that particular project.

2. Likewise, where a client employs the same organizations to plan, design, manage and construct a series of similar facilities, whether they be built sequentially or at the same time, the precise make-up of each team will vary. In this situation, some team members may move from project to project, taking their knowledge and experience with them. However, they will invariably be joined by others for whom the site, construction techniques and team composition represent a new challenge.

3. All projects, by definition, are temporary work places - even when they take place within an existing permanent facility.

4. Also, within the limited lifespan of the job, a large proportion of the team will only be involved for a part of the development programme.

THINK POINT:
ALL construction projects are 'one-offs'.

AND THERE'S SOMETHING EVEN MORE IMPORTANT

Common construction problems such as delays, cost over-runs, major defects and excessive snagging can eventually be resolved, accommodated or even forgotten. But there is another major issue in Construction that has much more significant and longer lasting effects.....

HUMAN MISERY

Health & Safety failings often leave a legacy of pain, suffering and human misery that can last a lifetime. The traditional measure of Health and Safety performance in Construction has been the rate of fatal injury – that is the number of people dying directly as a result of accidents associated with construction activities – published by the Health and Safety Executive (HSE) on an annual basis.

Historically, the number of fatal injuries has fallen from more than 250 deaths in the early 1960s to an average of fewer than 75 in recent years. As can be seen from Figure 2, both the number and rate of fatal injuries has dropped significantly over the last 35 years.

It is clear from looking at Fig. 2 that there has been a long downward trend in the number of fatal injuries suffered by construction workers since the 1960's and an even greater fall in the rate of fatal injury (i.e. the number of fatalities per 100,000 workers in the industry in that year).

However, although each fatality represents a disaster and a tragedy for those directly involved, they represent only the tip of an ice-berg of pain, suffering, physical, financial and emotional loss which continues to afflict many thousands of construction workers (as well as hundreds of members of the public) every year, as a result of management failure and human error.

Year	Number of deaths (approx)	Rate/100,000 workers (total annual workforce)
1969/70	260	N/A
1973/74	195	16.0 (1.2 million workers)
1979/80	125	11.8 (1.06 million)
1984/85	145	9.8 (1.47 million)
1989/90	140	9.4 (1.5 million)
1994/95	85	6.9 (1.23 million)
1999/2000	85	5.5 (1.54 million)
2004/05	65	3.5 (1.8 million)
2009/10	45	2.0 (2.0 million)

FIG 2: WORKPLACE FATALITIES IN CONSTRUCTION (SOURCE – HSE)

In a typical year (and most years are fairly typical) construction and ex-construction workers will suffer:-

- 800-900 deaths as a result of contracting an asbestos related disease
- 3500-4000 reported serious injuries (in fact, the 'true' number of serious injuries is estimated to be at least double the reported figures.)
- 80,000 – 100,000 cases of work related ill-health.

In addition, several members of the public will die and hundreds will be seriously injured by construction activities that go wrong.

THINK POINT:
There is a lot of emphasis on 'safety' in construction but how much on 'health'?

THINGS ARE GETTING BETTER – AREN'T THEY?

There have been significant changes in the way construction projects are managed and risks controlled over the past fifty years. In the 1960s the industry was more labour intensive with the majority of workers being directly employed by the main contractors carrying out the works.

Health and Safety legislation was minimal and concepts of what constituted acceptable risk were very different from today, not only in Construction but throughout society. In the intervening decades, increased mechanization, use of sub-contract labour and, more recently, off-site fabrication have had a significant impact on productivity, quality and safety performance.

The enactment of the Health and Safety at Work Act in 1974 was a significant point in time in creating a safer working environment. However, it is worth noting that the steepest fall in the number of fatal injuries in construction took place in the ten years preceding the act. From 1963/64 to 1975/76 deaths per year fell from 250 to around 150.

In the period from the mid 1970s to 1990 the annual rate fluctuated considerably but by 1991 the number of fatalities was still around 150 per year. Since then there has been a gradual decline in workplace deaths to the current level.

One of the questions that must be asked is:

"How much lower can we expect the figure to go?"

and this leads to a further question:

"What should we be doing to reduce the figure further?"

Looking purely numerically at the situation, it would appear that improvements in the way the industry conducts its affairs have delivered significant gains over the last few years. However, it would be simplistic to view the construction industry as an amorphous mass. The Construction Sector is actually made up of a number of sub-sectors which operate in different ways and have quite different attitudes to risk and varying levels of management competence.

DIFFERENT SECTORS, DIFFERENT PROBLEMS

Engineering Construction is predominantly involved with the design, construction and maintenance of process plants across the oil and gas, power generation, steel, chemical and petrochemical sectors as well as industries such as nuclear waste reprocessing, pharmaceutical, cement, glass, paper, food, brewing and distillation.

Engineering Construction in the UK currently employs around 60,000 people, primarily in repair and maintenance activities. However, in coming years, new-build projects, particularly in the energy sector will become an increasingly significant part of the overall workload.

Civil Engineering covers that part of the industry involved with the design, construction and maintenance of infrastructure works such as bridges, roads, railways, dams, water treatment and distribution facilities, airports and tunnels. Although civil engineering works can be found in most categories of construction activity, civil engineering projects are typically characterized by a high level of management competence as well as technical appreciation. Failures on such projects, (e.g. Can Tho Bridge, see below) can be spectacular and lead to high numbers of fatalities, although this is rare in the UK.

CAN THO BRIDGE COLLAPSE

Failure of falsework supporting a newly poured concrete deck on the US$300 million Can Tho bridge in Vietnam caused a catastrophic collapse in October 2007. An 87m long section of the 2.75km long concrete deck – two spans of the approach structure leading to the cable-stayed bridge over the Hau (Bassac) River in the Mekong delta – fell after the 30m-high scaffolding support system gave way. At the time of the collapse, 250 people were working on and under the failed section, which had been poured the previous day. 54 people died and 80 others were injured.

An eight month enquiry concluded that the sinking of a makeshift foundation framework was the main cause of the collapse.

General Construction covers a wide range of commercial, retail, leisure, industrial and residential (though not traditional housing) developments typically involving a broad spectrum of professional and trade expertise including architects, consulting engineers, building services consultants, general and specialist contractors. Projects may involve complete new build, extensions to existing facilities or refurbishment and structural modification of existing buildings. Levels of competence and scope of duties can differ widely depending on the size and nature of the project and even for smaller projects can involve a large number of contributors, with very different cultures and levels of involvement in delivering a successful project.

House-building involves predominantly traditional building techniques. Projects can range from developments of a few dwellings carried out by local builders/developers to multi-million pound developments carried out by national house-building companies. Designs of such buildings are often standardized, and construction work, even on large scale projects, may be carried out by trade contractors with limited management and technical capabilities.

Facilities Management (FM) – is a relatively modern concept primarily devoted to the maintenance and care of commercial or institutional buildings, such as hotels, hospitals, schools, office complexes etc. Clients who do not wish to carry out non-core functions with their own personnel contract a variety of duties to an FM contractor who will typically use a combination of their own staff together with sub-contracted workers to carry out routine operational functions. Duties may include the care of air conditioning, electric power, plumbing and lighting systems; cleaning; decoration; grounds maintenance and security. These duties are referred to as non-core or support services, because they are not the primary business (taken in the broadest sense of the word) of the owner organization. Health and safety problems are typically much less an issue than the other sectors

Domestic Building is a largely unregulated sector which carries out minor building and refurbishment works for individuals and small businesses. A disproportionate number of fatalities and serious injuries occur in this sector; under-reporting of serious injuries is a major problem and ignorance of legal obligations is widespread. Enforcement action is common but the impact on other organizations is very limited. Falls from height, or falls through fragile roofs, and electrocution of unqualified workers, feature heavily in the statistics.

Over the period 2002-2007, the majority of fatal injuries were attributed to domestic, house-building and repair and refurbishment operations, with relatively few occurring on major construction sites. However, more recently there has been a spate of fatalities on sites operated by major contractors which have called into question the risk management strategies adopted by the "top tier" of construction organisations.

FIG 3: CONSTRUCTION INDUSTRY SUB-SECTORS

PAPERING OVER THE CRACKS!

In recent years, risk management in Construction has increasingly focused on paper based risk assessment procedures and mandatory wearing of evermore items of personal protective equipment, often driven by advice from qualified Health and Safety practitioners – either in-house advisers or external consultants.

Many people working in Construction assume that these approaches are driven by legal requirements. However, a review of the key legislation relating to developing safe systems of work in construction paints a very different picture.

So let's have a quick look at what the law actually says.

THE HEALTH AND SAFETY AT WORK ACT 1974

As the first industrial nation in the world, it is not surprising that the UK developed the earliest concepts of occupational health and safety obligations enshrined in law.

As early as 1802 the Health and Morals of Apprentices Act laid down certain minimum standards for young people working in cotton mills (at this time children as young as five years old could be found working in mills and factories.), as well as minimum basic standards for workplace cleanliness and ventilation. Subsequent Factories Acts, culminating in the Factory Act of 1878 formed a foundation for subsequent workplace Health and Safety legislation, leading eventually to the HASAWA 1974.

It is important to understand the fundamental shift in approach which the Health & Safety at Work Act ushered in. Up until 1974 the Victorian approach to workplace legislation was maintained – narrow regulatory standards were formulated on an empirical basis, for particular categories of workers in relation to specific industries, initially factories and mills, which employed large numbers of workers in perceptibly dangerous environments.

This piecemeal approach continued in the twentieth century as other industries came to the attention of the legislators, e.g.

- Mines & Quarries Act 1954
- Factories Act 1961
- Office, Shops and Railway Premises Act 1963
- Nuclear Installations Act 1965

The first regulations specific to Construction were implemented in the early 1960's:-

- The Construction (General Provision) Regulations 1961
- The Construction (Lifting Operations) Regulations 1961
- The Construction (Working Places) Regulations 1966
- The Construction (Health & Welfare) Regulations 1966

However, for millions of workers outside these particular industries, the law afforded no statutory protection until HASAWA 1974 came into effect on 31st July 1974.

The Act was ambitious in its scope but deceptively simple in its approach. It set out to define the general principles for creating a safe place and systems of work that could be applied to any workplace in the UK, irrespective of the nature of the work, number of employees or type of premises.

Being an "enabling Act", it allowed for further legislation, known as "Statutory Instruments" or more commonly "Regulations", to be made, without recourse to the full Parliamentary process. These regulations could provide detailed standards for particular work situations.

The Act was a well thought out piece of legislation and an examination of the provisions of the Act demonstrates that all the main requirements for managing occupational safety and health were identified. Subsequent regulations simply serve to reinforce and elaborate on these requirements.

THE CONCEPT OF DUTYHOLDERS

The Act employed the concept of identifying a number of dutyholders with specific duties, who were expected to work *together* in order to create a safe place of work. Unfortunately this concept has led to some confusion as to "who has to do what?"

The five duty holder functions defined in the Act are:-

- Employers (and managers)
- Employees
- Self-employed
- Designers, manufacturers & suppliers of articles and substances
- Controllers of premises

The term "Dutyholder" describes a function, not an individual. So for example, the owner of a factory will have both the duties of an employer (towards his employees) and a controller of premises (to anybody visiting his premises).

Depending on what the factory produces he may also be classed as a 'Designer, manufacturer or supplier...'

Let's consider these duties as they relate to a Construction environment:-

Employers have the most numerous specific duties which can be split into two distinct categories:

Duties in relation to the Workplace:

- provide & maintain a safe place of work including access & egress
- provision and maintenance of safe plant and systems of work
- arrangements for the safe use, handling, storage and transport of articles and substances
- provision and maintenance of a safe environment with adequate welfare facilities.

Duties in relation to People:

- provide information, instruction and training to employees and others (e.g. contractors) to enable them to carry out their work safely.
- ensure that workers are effectively supervised so that safe systems of work are adhered to
- consultation with the workforce on matters of health and safety

Employees have specific duties to work in a responsible manner:-

- taking reasonable care so as not to risk themselves or other people who may be affected by their actions (or omissions)
- co-operate with their employer on matters of health & safety

Self-employed have broadly the same duties as employees.

It is worth noting that in the eyes of the Law anybody working in a client's business undertaking whether directly employed or engaged on some other terms, will be viewed effectively as an employee for the duration of their working under that employer's control.

Designers, manufacturers and suppliers of <u>articles</u> have duties to:-

- ensure, as far as they can, that they are designed and constructed so as to be safe (including testing where necessary)
- ensure adequate information is supplied for their use
- take steps to provide revisions of information if a serious risk to health or safety becomes known

The duties in relation to manufacturers and suppliers of <u>substances</u> are broadly similar.

Controllers of premises (who may be the client, principal contractor or facilities management company) have a duty to:-

- anybody not in their employment, to ensure as far as they can that the premises, all means of access and egress, and any plant or substances in the premises are safe to use.

Unfortunately the construction industry was slow to respond to the requirements of the Act, and standards of, and attitudes to health and safety changed only slowly through the 1970's and 80's.

It is arguable that this state of affairs would have continued but for the European Community Framework Directive which, in 1989, introduced measures to encourage improvements in the safety and health of workers at work. In the UK, the provisions of the Directive were implemented through the Management of Health and Safety at Work Regulations in 1992.

MANAGEMENT OF HEALTH AND SAFETY AT WORK REGULATIONS 1999

The original regulations (revised in 1999) made explicit the requirement to identify hazards, and assess risk as part of the process for developing safe systems of work. This approach was fundamentally different from previous UK legislation, which with its origins in specific industrial situations, had tended to be prescriptive, defining what must be done in all situations.

By contrast the 'European' approach was to acknowledge that it is impossible to legislate for every eventuality and combination of circumstances, and instead placed the onus on those organising a work activity to consider what might go wrong, and to put in place measures that they considered would reduce the risk of harm to an acceptably low level.

The Management Regulations also required that *"the significant findings"* from this *"risk assessment process"* should be recorded, in a format that would be retrievable at a later date.

These regulations do not require this to be in writing (or refer to the production of method statements) as part of the risk assessment process. However, since 1999 there has been a massive growth in the amount of paperwork generated on construction projects, allegedly "to meet our legal obligations."

There is no doubt that the Management Regulations have had a huge influence in the way construction organizations systematically deal with health and safety.

It is easy to overlook the fact that these regulations, like the Health & Safety at Work Act 1974, are 'general' legislation, applying to all workplaces, and all employees, irrespective of the nature of activities being carried out in the workplace.

Unlike most other work activities, construction is by its' nature temporary, transient and, at times, unpredictable - and this makes it a far greater management challenge than most other sectors.

The 'standard' approach to risk assessment suggested by the Management Regulations was not well suited to a dynamic, ever changing work place, where the majority of the workforce could be classified as *"temporary workers"* or *"persons working in host employers' undertakings".*

It is hardly surprising then, that within two years of the Management Regulations taking effect (in 1993), the construction sector was provided with a bespoke version of the regulations, specifically tailored to meet the needs of a project based work environment.

The Construction (Design & Management) Regulations 1994 (CDM) came into force on 31st March 1995.

CONSTRUCTION (DESIGN & MANAGEMENT) REGULATIONS 1994

The construction industry attitude to health and safety responsibility was very different prior to the introduction of the CDM (1994) regulations. Sir Michael Latham's report "Constructing the Team", published in July 1994, had been commissioned by the UK Government following a series of poorly performing high profile public sector projects. The main focus of the report was how projects were procured and the contractual arrangements being employed at the time. The report described the construction sector of that period as *"ineffective", "adversarial", "fragmented", "incapable of delivering for its customers",* and *"lacking respect for its employees".*

The rate of fatal injury in 1994 was between 5 and 5.5 per 100,000 workers (around 100 fatal accidents per year). At this time accidents and injuries on site were viewed as exclusively the responsibility of the contractors involved (main contractors and where relevant their sub-contractors).

Investigations by the HSE tended to focus on the circumstances directly contributing to the incident i.e. the <u>primary</u> causes of the accident.

The CDM 1994 regulations ushered in a radically different approach to providing safer systems of work for both the contractors of engineered facilities and those who would come after – during maintenance, modification and ultimately, demolition of the structures. Accidents, rather than simply being the result of acts or omissions by the workers involved, were now viewed as being (partly, at least) the consequence of decisions taken earlier in the design and construction process by people who had not previously considered health and safety their responsibility. Decisions by the client and their advisers on what to build, how much they were willing to spend, and the programme duration allowable for the completion of the project were now viewed as having a bearing on the attitudes and behaviour of the construction workforce.

Likewise, the scheme designers – architects, structural engineers, process and building services designers, individually and in collaboration – were considered to have the capacity to reduce exposure to high risk situations of both the construction workforce and subsequently those carrying out maintenance and repair work on the facility.

In the design of "articles" (i.e. components of the building or structure) consideration was to be given, for example, to reducing the amount of work at height, the need for manual handling of large components, and eliminating works which require tools for drilling, breaking and scabbling that could expose workers to excessive vibration.

In the specification of "substances" – chemical compounds such as concrete and mortar additives, paints and other coatings etc – designers were expected to assess possible damaging effects on human health and consider substitutions with less harmful products, subject to quality considerations.

CDM brought a major change in how construction health and safety was perceived, making the client's and designer's duties explicit for the first time. As these regulations, unlike the Management Regulations (1999), were written specifically for Construction, the language used in the Regulations and Approved Code of Practice (ACOP) should have been more comprehensible.

However, from the out-set the intentions of the CDM Regulations became a muddle in the minds of many in the industry.

THINK POINT:
Are *you* clear about your obligations under CDM?

DUTYHOLDERS UNDER CDM 1994

As with the HASAWA 1974, the CDM Regulations identified five duty holders. For the construction environment the duty holders were defined as:

- Client
- Designers
- Planning Supervisor
- Principal Contractor
- Contractor

Although the specific duties of these dutyholders were spelt out in some detail in the Regulations, the <u>process</u> by which hazards were to be eliminated and risks reduced during the development of the design of the works was not clearly addressed.

PAPERWORK, PAPERWORK, PAPERWORK

The creation of the function "Planning Supervisor" was intended to ensure that:

*"**those who carry out design work on a project, particularly during the design phase, collaborate and pay adequate attention to the need to reduce risk wherever possible**".*

In addition the Planning Supervisor was required to:-

- ensure that a pre-tender, or pre-construction health and safety plan is prepared in good time
- ensure that a health and safety plan is prepared, reviewed and amended as necessary and given to the client

These two "documents" were each intended to serve an important purpose.

The Pre-tender health and safety plan:

In 1994, particularly in the public sector, the main method of procurement of contracts was by competitive tender with (typically) up to six contractors submitting sealed bids pricing the work against detailed drawings and bills of quantities. It was not normal for health and safety to be identified as an item to be priced. Rather, contractors included, at their own discretion, an allowance within their rates for whatever health and safety measures they deemed appropriate.

As clients were obliged to accept the lowest bid (except in the most exceptional circumstances) there was considerable pressure on estimators to pare down costs to a minimum, putting severe pressure on allowances for health, safety and welfare provision.

Information supplied by the Client within the pre-tender health and safety plan was intended to ensure that all contractors were pricing for the same risk items, thus providing "a level playing field" and reducing the likelihood that the contractor who failed to make adequate cost provision for health and safety would win the contract.

The Health and Safety file:

This was intended to provide information needed during future construction works, **"which includes cleaning, maintenance, alterations, refurbishment and demolition"**. The content of the file was intended to "be available to occupiers, maintenance personnel and future designers to" alert them to risks and help them to decide how to work safely.

In both cases, the tendency of Planning Supervisors and others was to value quantity of information over quality. Rather than identify specific information that was valuable and necessary to other members of the project team, a common approach was to "err on the side of caution" and include much information that related to the project in some way – but did not assist team members in developing effective risk control measures.

The result was that very little useful information about risk filtered down to the people at the 'sharp end'– the Contractors.

THINK POINT:
The law doesn't ask for lots of paperwork, and Personal Protective Equipment (PPE) should be considered a last resort – so how have we ended up with masses of both?

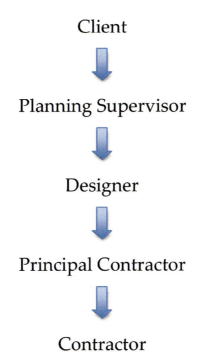

FIG 4: THE COMMUNICATION CHAIN – CDM 1994

THERE ARE DESIGNERS, AND DESIGNERS

Perhaps one of the most confusing aspects of the CDM 1994 regulations related to the duties and function of "Designers".

In CDM the term "Designer" has a much wider meaning than is commonly understood. In addition to architects, civil and structural engineers, building surveyors, landscape architects and design practices the term in the Approved Code Of Practice (ACOP) covered :-

- anyone who specifies or alters a design, or who specifies the use of a particular method of work or material e.g. a quantity surveyor who insists on a specific material or a client who stipulates a particular layout for a new production building
- building services designers, engineering practices or others designing fixed plant from which people can fall more than 2 metres

- those purchasing materials where the choice has been left open
- contractors carrying out design work as part of their contribution to a project
- temporary works engineers including those designing formwork, falsework, scaffolding and sheet piling.

In simple terms, the Regulations imply that there are <u>primary</u> designers whose main role is to develop design aspects of the project, and <u>secondary</u> designers, i.e. any other member of the project team who at some point makes a decision that could have implications for those constructing, cleaning or using the building.

THINK POINT:
The regulations, make ***no distinction*** in the duties of these two quite different groups.

The response of the industry in general, to this significant aspect of the CDM Regulations was slow and muddled. As late as 2003, a HSE survey found that only 8% of designers had taken any formal training in their responsibilities under CDM regulations.

Research by Loughborough University into the causes of site accidents suggested in around 50% of the incidents studied, design changes would have mitigated the accident. Unfortunately many of the staff working in design offices have little involvement with, or understanding of construction operations and the site conditions in which their designs will be turned into reality.

PRINCIPAL CONTRACTORS AND CONTRACTORS

Initially it appeared that CDM 1994 imposed little in the way of additional duties on the contractors engaged in constructing the works. The duties of the Principal Contractor were largely in line with what the main contractor would have been expected to do prior to the introduction of the regulations. Likewise, contractors were only expected to co-operate with the Principal Contractor and comply with their legal obligations under HASAWA and associated regulations (e.g. RIDDOR).

Perhaps the most significant, if subtle change, was the change in relationship between the 'main' contractor and others working on the site – whether it be their own sub-contractors, utilities, or people working directly for the client.

"Contractors" within the definition of the regulations were expected to take responsibility for the management of their own operations, rather than simply providing a workforce to work under the direct control of the main contractor.

The Principal Contractor was empowered to require all contractors to:-

- supply details of their work and any risks to others created by it
- provide their employees with information and training
- consult their workers on matters of health and safety
- comply with site safety rules

The aim of the regulations was to create a culture on site where everyone was working together in a co-ordinated way, with a clear focus on minimising the risk to construction workers and members of the public.

DROWNING IN PAPER?

There is no doubt that the CDM 1994 Regulations played a key role in elevating the management of risk to a formal, systematic level. Unfortunately, the tendency to equate the production of paperwork with improved risk management took hold very quickly.

Despite protestations by the HSE, it gradually became the norm to demand "risk assessments and method statements" for all activities carried out on site. It is difficult to establish how this situation arose – it certainly was not a requirement of the Regulations.

The only reference to method statements appeared in section 182 of the ACOP:-

> "**All contractors must....provide information to the Principal Contractor about risks to others created by their work. This information might, for example, come from risk assessments and method statements**".

A huge bureaucracy has grown up in Construction, where the production of documents, defining down to the last detail how a job will be done safely, has replaced the practical, team based risk assessment that was intended.

THINK POINT:
For the revised CDM 2007 Regulations the HSE adopted a slogan: '**Teamwork, not paperwork**' – yet on most projects there are still huge amounts of paperwork - why do you think this is?

SECTION 1 REVIEW

- Fragmentation of the team: a failure to work as a coherent unit - is at the heart of most failure in Construction.

- All construction projects are 'one-offs'.

- The fatality rate is not a good measure of health and safety in the Construction sector. It ignores serious injuries and doesn't take into account health-related deaths or ill-health.

- Under the CDM Regulations, a designer is anyone who specifies or alters a design, or who specifies the use of a particular method of work or material

- Just producing more paperwork will not make projects work better or more safely.

- The key to successful projects is to build the team first.

SECTION 2

UNDERSTANDING
CDM

IN WHICH WE EXPLORE:

The detail of the legislation

The implications for members of the construction team

The real requirements of the law

'Teamwork not Paperwork.'

The guiding principles underpinning the CDM Regulations have not changed since they were introduced in 1994. The original Regulations made explicit for those involved in construction work, the general duties contained within the Health and Safety at Work Act (HASAWA) 1974 and the Management of Health and Safety at Work Regulations (MHSWR) 1992.

Because they were sector specific, the CDM Regulations could address the management of risk during the construction process with a greater focus than was possible with the HASAWA and MHSWR (due to their wider application to all workplaces).

In summary CDM 1994 required:-

- a realistic programme with adequate time allowed for planning, preparation and the work itself
- early appointment of key people
- competent duty holders with sufficient resources to meet their legal duties
- early identification and reduction of risks
- provision of health and safety information from the start of the design phase, through construction and maintenance, to eventual demolition
- co-operation between duty holders
- effort and resources proportionate to the risk and complexity of the project to be applied to managing health and safety issues.

THINK POINT:
It was never intended that risk management become a paperwork exercise and the HSE took every opportunity to explain this to the Industry.

Unfortunately, a combination of ignorance to the real aims of CDM, and the desire to have an "audit trail" should legal action result from management failure, led to paperwork being demanded and produced with very little thought being given to the significant risk issues.

Possibly the worst manifestation of this phenomenon was the proliferation of "generic risk assessments" – a self-contradictory term if ever there was one! To carry out a meaningful risk assessment you must take into account all the factors pertaining to that specific scenario at that particular time. Whilst there may be known hazards which will always be present when carrying out a particular operation (and therefore could be termed generic), other factors will vary from situation to situation. The risk assessment must take into account both the "generic" and 'variable' factors if it is to be deemed "**suitable and sufficient**".

For example, an operation placing in-situ concrete will always involve the risk of chromate burns should the operative's skin come into contact with the wet concrete. This is a generic hazard associated with concreting operations. Other factors, such as method of placing of the concrete, types of equipment used, location, weather conditions etc will all combine to produce a unique situation that cannot be addressed through a "generic" approach.

THINK POINT:
There is **no such thing** as a generic risk assessment.

Perhaps influenced by the same orthodox thinking, designers often adopted a similar approach to contractors when considering risk management. Although there was no specific requirement for a Design Risk Assessment (DRA) in the CDM Regulations, the production of design risk assessment paperwork, often generic and focusing on site rather than the design issues, became increasingly common.

Shortly before the consultation began for the revised Regulations in 2005, the HSE produced some guidelines on the issue. Under the heading "CDM – Designers Can Do More", the HSE stated:-

- The Construction (Design and Management) Regulations are 10 years old – but despite time, effort, money and forests of paper there is plenty of evidence that the designer aspects are still not working well.
- Research shows that designers are still failing to exploit the potential they have to eliminate and reduce risks on site.
- HSE interventions with designers show that designers are often uncertain of their responsibilities, lack information and training, and produce mountains of generic DRA paperwork that adds little value, and;
- Lets face it, the wording of the designer legislation is far from easy, so that's a job for HSE to sort out.

The HSE view of Construction's response to the CDM Regulations was based not only on its own experience of dealing with the Industry but detailed research carried out by independent consultants, looking at various aspects of the application of the Regulation, including the following reports (all of which are available on the HSE website):

- RR148 - The Case for CDM better safer design – a pilot study
- RR306 - Investigating practices in communication and information exchange amongst CDM dutyholders
- RR467 - The Commercial Case for Applying CDM
- RR538 - Improving the effectiveness of the Construction (Design & Management) Regulations 1994

Report RR467 is particularly pointed in its criticism. In section 1.4, Summary of Issues Affecting Designers, it states:-

"The requirements of CDM Regulations 13, which relate to the duties of designers, have not, in our opinion been effectively managed by some parts of industry. We have identified the following contributory reasons:

- Many designers have little knowledge or no understanding of the body of health and safety law and its purpose to prevent accidents and ill health. HSE surveys of designers have shown that few design practices have understood the need to extend training beyond CDM wording. It is not possible to deliver CDM without a wider understanding of legal requirements;
- Many designers have had no interest in the potential contribution they could make. Some designers continue to try to evade responsibility, to ignore their duties and to waste the opportunities presented to add value;
- Many designers have had little involvement with practical site processes and have real difficulty in understanding the significant differences between clean lines on drawings and the reality of sites, structures and structural elements. A frightening number of young designers have not given any consideration to how large, awkward or heavy structural elements are to be placed nor the contribution the design team can make to facilitate such processes".

This report also concurred with the HSE view that the wording of the legislation had contributed to the existing state of affairs, including the following contributory factors:

- "The wording of the regulation is insufficiently precise to set standards in relation to legal duties.
- The definition of designer and design is not that which is generally accepted by Industry. It includes many who would be horrified to discover that they could be considered to be designers by a strict legal interpretation."

In an attempt to address these concerns and to respond to issues arising from the HSE's 2002 Discussion Document "Revitalising Health and Safety in Construction", the Health and Safety Commission (HSC) issued proposals aimed at simplifying the CDM regulations in March 2005 and launched a four month on-line consultation with the intent of bringing the revised regulation into force in October 2006.

In addition to making the basic requirements clearer and more comprehensible the proposals aimed to:

- maximise flexibility to fit in with a wide range of different contractual arrangements
- strengthen the requirements for co-ordination and co-operation – <u>particularly between designers and contractors</u>
- encourage integrated working between the project team members
- simplify the process for assessing competence.

In addition, it was proposed that the new regulations include duties which had previously been contained within the Construction (Health, Safety and Welfare) Regulations. Thus there was to be one set of Construction regulations embracing all aspects of the design and construction process that would improve the management of risk by virtue of the fact that dutyholders could *"easily identify and understand their own role (and those of other members of the project team)"*.

The Regulations were delayed by several months but shortly before they came into effect on April 2007 the HSE made this pronouncement:

THINK POINT:
'Construction remains a **disproportionately dangerous** industry where **improvements** in health and safety **are urgently needed**'.

The initial response of the industry suggests that the HSE view was not shared by many in the industry. From clients to material producers there were cries of "unfair". The Forum for Private Business even lobbied the Conservative Party to table a debate in the House of Commons in an attempt to overturn the legislation.

NEW REGULATION, NEW FOCUS

What were the changes which caused such a furore in some quarters? Although the CDM 2007 regulations largely reinforce and amplify the message in CDM 94 there were a number of significant changes.

The Client

The new regulations removed the role of Client's Agent. Under CDM 94 the client could *'appoint a competent, adequately resourced agent to carry out their CDM duties',* although the ACOP went on to state *'but they retain their other duties under health & safety law such as ensuring the health and safety of people affected by their work.'* This was viewed by many clients as an opportunity to 'contract out' their responsibilities and, in effect, walk away from both their moral and legal obligations.

The new regulations sought to emphasise the findings of a study carried out in 1998 for the Norwegian State Oil Company which found that –

THINK POINT:
'Construction projects with a good health and safety record were those in which the **client** was the **principal driver** of best health and safety practice.'

Whilst it was acknowledged that clients cannot be expected to have the knowledge and skills to manage a construction project themselves the ACOP suggests that *'the client has one of the biggest influences on the way the project is run.'*

'He who pays the piper calls the tune' - you might say.

The decisions, attitude and business culture of the client have a major bearing on how the project develops and to which aspects of the project delivery the construction team pay most attention. It is the client who:-

- determines the time money and other resources available for the project
- selects the key members of the project team
- chooses the contractual arrangements
- sets the culture which can encourage collaborative working or promote divisive, partisan relationships amongst the project team.

Although CDM applies to all projects deemed to involve 'construction work', client duties become more onerous if the project is '*notifiable.*'

Apart from domestic clients (that is, people having work done on their own homes), clients of even small scale construction works are obliged to comply with 'Part 2 – General Management Duties Applying to Construction Projects' which impose basic duties on clients, designers and contractors. If a project is expected to last longer than thirty days or involve more than 500 person days of normal working (for example 50 people working for longer than ten days) the HSE must be notified at the earliest possible opportunity, using the HSE notification document known as an F10.

Clearly some clients will be ignorant of these requirements until they are advised of their legal obligations. The regulations require that any designer involved in the early stages of the development of a project must check that the client is aware of these duties.

If the project is notifiable the client is required to appoint a CDM co-ordinator to orchestrate the risk management process and ensure that health and safety considerations are at the forefront of everybody's thinking, particularly in the early stages of the project, when key decisions can critically affect the subsequent conditions in which people will be required to work.

The CDM co-ordinator function, which can be treated either as a stand alone role or combined with another project function, replaced that of the Planning Supervisor under CDM 94, a role that had largely become discredited, having been generally perceived as ineffectual and focussed more on bureaucracy than risk reduction.

The CDM co-ordinator
The ACOP describes the role as '**to provide the client with a key project advisor in respect of construction health and safety risk management matters**' and summarises the main duties:

> '*They should assist and advise the client on appointment of competent contractors and the adequacy of management arrangements, ensure proper co-ordination of the health and safety aspects of the design process, facilitate good communication and co-operation between project team members and prepare the health and safety file.*'

The intention in creating this role, in place of the Planning Supervisor, was to provide an empowered and pivotal figure who could assist the client in selecting and shaping competent construction professionals into a cohesive and effective team.

In the consultative document, circulated prior to finalising the new regulations, the HSC stated:-

'We have not lost sight of the fact that good health and safety has commercial benefits too - better quality and more chance of the project being completed on time and coming in on budget because the site will be better managed. We see the co-ordinator as being instrumental in ensuring this.'

Unfortunately, perhaps as a legacy of the ill-fated Planning Supervisor role, the CDM co-ordinator is often viewed as a low profile administrator whose prime role is to compile the health and safety file, and who plays little, if any, part in the dynamic process of risk reduction through collaboration between the client and their designers and contractors.

THINK POINT:
Think about projects in which you are involved – **what does the CDM co-ordinator do?**

It is precisely because clients cannot reasonably be expected to have the knowledge and understanding of construction to manage the process themselves that the CDM co-ordinator role was created. To fulfil the role effectively requires a broad range of capabilities including:-

- good interpersonal skill in order to encourage other members of the project team to work in an open and collaborative manner.
- sound understanding of the health and safety issues which will need to be addressed and the principles underpinning CDM and associated legislation.
- an appreciation of the design process and an ability to build rapport with designers.
- an ability to identify where knowledge and understanding is lacking and promote a culture of knowledge sharing and mutual support within the project team.

By removing the client's agent role, the revised regulations require the client to take a closer interest in the project to ensure that various fundamental requirements are in place to protect and benefit the workforce. With the support of an empowered and knowledgeable CDM co-ordinator, any client should be clear as to what they have to do, and what they can expect from other competent members of the project team.

For example, the regulations specifically require that adequate welfare facilities be in place from the very beginning of the construction phase. The client does not have to provide them (normally the Principal Contractor would do this) but if there are particular constraints the client should co-operate with contractors and assist them with their arrangements. This may involve providing access to temporary electrical or water supplies, or even the short term use of existing toilet and rest facilities. A client who shows some concern for the welfare of site workers can expect a greater commitment from their construction team in return.

It is regrettable that such situations are often viewed purely in terms of 'What are our legal obligations?' Over and above any prescribed legal obligations there is a moral duty on everyone to show respect and consideration for other people affected by our actions. If we adopt an attitude of complying with the spirit as well as the letter of the law we may find promoting health and safety a less arduous task. Because of the complex technical, contractual and commercial issues that have to be managed there is a tendency for projects to become 'dehumanised' – decisions are based on 'hard nosed' considerations without all the pertinent factors being taken into account. Over and above the 'technical' aspects of the scheme, a project is a human undertaking where co-operation, co-ordination and effective two-way communication are critical to successful outcomes for the client and their project team.

Unfortunately, many people in the industry with well developed technical and commercial skills have poor interpersonal skills and find it difficult to relate to other members of the project team. This invariably has consequences for how risk management issues are addressed.

Designers
CDM 2007 failed to address the confusion arising from the conflation of the 'scheme' or 'primary' designers with other members of the project team (including the client, commercial or purchasing professionals, contractors etc.) who may make or contribute to decisions of a design nature as part of their involvement with the project.

For the sake of clarity, this section will focus on the duties of designers whose prime role is to carry out design work associated with the project and who would readily recognise themselves when scrutinising the duties of designers set out in the ACOP.

At first glance the duties of designers appear largely unchanged from the original regulations but whereas CDM 94 stated:-

'Designers responsibilities extend beyond the construction phase of a project. They also need to consider the health and safety of those who will maintain, repair, clean and eventually demolish the structure.'

CDM 2007 goes further:-

'Designers responsibilities extend beyond the construction phase of a project. They also need to consider the health and safety of those who will maintain repair, clean, refurbish and eventually remove or demolish all or part of a structure as well as the health and safety of users of the workplace.'

The next part of the statement is questionable, given the findings of HSE research carried out around the time that the regulations were being redrafted:-

'For most designers, buildability considerations and ensuring that the structure can be easily maintained and repaired will be part of the normal work, and thinking about the health and safety of those who do this work should not be an onerous duty.'

We would suggest that most designers are specialists in one area of the design of a facility or building and will have limited understanding of other design disciplines engaged on the same project. For example an architect, structural engineer and building services engineer all design particular aspects of the same building, but with very different technical knowledge and expertise. The final building design is the result of combining the three components that could loosely be described as the building fabric, the building structure and the building services. If each designer works separately, it is difficult to see how they could assess their impact not only on construction personnel but the end users/occupiers of the completed building.

It seems evident to us that whilst each can risk asses their designs as they progress, only by collaborating with each other and consulting other parties with relevant experience (such as contractors, maintenance workers, end users) can they hope to demonstrate that risks have been reduced to an acceptable level. It is this collaboration which can yield not only safer structures but also more efficient and innovative designs that will serve the client better in the long term.

The ACOP cites a very good example of this effect:-

"On a major office development with a large central atrium, the electrical contractor highlighted an innovative product for the roof glazing that was unknown to the other team members, including the designers. This was a double glazed unit incorporating internal prismatic reflectors. It removed the problem of glare and the need for high level roller blinds. It was virtually maintenance free, and led to significant savings over the life of the building, and significantly reduced the need to work at height."

THE THREE C'S

This example sums up the true meaning of "the three C's":

- Communication
- Co-operation
- Co-ordination

Clearly there are many factors to be evaluated when considering an innovative design change such as the one above, including performance, cost and reliability of unfamiliar products. The law requires that we at least consider different ways of designing and do not simply default to the traditional solutions that we know, in some cases, contribute to unhealthy and dangerous practices.

COMPETENCE

Whilst the previous CDM Regulations legislation required dutyholders to assess the competence of those they appoint CDM 2007 goes further, with potentially serious consequences for clients, designers and contractors involved in a major incident.

The new regulations reflect a concern expressed by many dutyholders that they were unsure how to assess for competence of those they appoint. There is more detailed guidance in the ACOP (appendix 4) to give those assessing competence a framework within which to work. Unfortunately, for many projects, this requirement consists of little more than a paper exercise demonstrating the written policies, arrangements and previous relevant experience of the organisation being assessed. It is obviously more time consuming and requires greater levels of skill to assess the individuals who will actually work on the project and this is a critical element of the assessment process which is often neglected. The dispersed nature of construction offers plenty of reasons why the specific individuals cannot be identified and/or made available during the assessment process.

THINK POINT:
A high-level assessment of an organisation's capabilities is insufficient to determine the competence of their people.

Competence can be summed up by:

Skills **K**nowledge **A**ttitude **T**raining & **E**xperience

Face to face interviews or, even better, discussions relating to the specific project risk issues are an essential part of establishing the suitability of the individuals being proposed. All the policies, procedures, training records etc supplied by most organisations are simply supporting evidence that should be demonstrated by the conduct of the assigned personnel.

As the ACOP states:-

'Remember that assessments should focus on the needs of the particular project and be proportionate to the risks, size and complexity of the work. Unnecessary bureaucracy associated with completing assessments can obscure the real issues and divert effort away from them.'

It must be remembered that 'competence' as referred to under CDM relates to their ability to meet their health and safety obligations rather than their technical role.

CDM 2007 also requires those taken on to do the work to ensure that they are competent to carry out the required tasks prior to accepting their appointment.

COMMON SENSE

We can see that at the heart of the CDM Regulations lies a common sense approach:

- Choose the project team members carefully
- Spend time at the very beginning of the project, agreeing how to work together.
- From the very start, work together to identify and minimise risk – and include everyone in the process
- Communicate clearly with each other throughout the project
- When things go wrong work together to find a solution

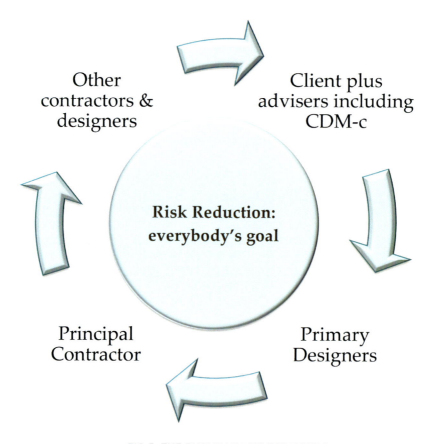

FIG 5: THE RISK MANAGEMENT TEAM

SECTION 2 REVIEW

- Construction remains a disproportionately dangerous industry where improvements in health and safety are "urgently needed".

- There is no such thing as a generic risk assessment.

- Construction projects with a good health and safety record were those in which the client was the principal driver of best health and safety practice.

- Designers have a key role in minimising risk in construction projects

- Individual members of the team cannot carry out their risk assessment duties effectively in isolation.

SECTION 3

FIRST BUILD
THE TEAM

IN WHICH WE LEARN:

The value of building the team early

What we need to do to comply with the law

The importance of the CDM Co-ordinator role

'We don't invent new ways of killing and injuring people in Construction – we use the tried and tested methods'

The performance of any project team is a function of the individual skills and attitudes of the people who make up the team, combined with the way they interact and co-ordinate their efforts to deliver the best results.

Construction project teams typically share a number of characteristics:-

- The team will not, in its entirety, have worked together before – even if some team members have.
- The team members will have different technical skills, knowledge and experience, only some of which will be relevant to the current project.
- Some of the team will be allocated to the project on a full time basis whilst others, particularly designers and professional advisers, may be working on two or more projects at the same time.
- The attitude of individual members when joining a new project team will be influenced by, amongst other things:-
    - their own personal character traits
    - the culture of the organisation that employs them
    - their position within the team
    - their perception of other team members
    - their experience of working in previous project teams
    - the degree of their involvement in the decision-making process affecting various aspects of the project.

It is a little regarded fact in much of the Industry that the performance of the team is a product of the contributions of every single member of that team.

Because of the way most projects develop, members tend to join (and leave) the team at different times, so that the organisation is in a constant state of flux. This is such a common feature of construction projects that the fact is accepted and the question is rarely raised:

'What can we do to ensure the effectiveness of the team as the project progresses through its various phases and personnel change?'

Many construction professionals can remember being part of only one or two teams that performed exceptionally well. In fact, the experience seems to be sufficiently infrequent that the features that made that team 'special' are rarely examined.

Although a considerable amount of research has been carried out into the characteristics of high performing teams in other sectors, construction teams tend to be unaware of the principles of team working and focus almost exclusively on the technical/commercial aspects and challenges of a project. Little or no attempt is made to maximize the effectiveness of the team through 'people-centred' work based activity.

The term 'team building event' is likely to conjure up an image of activities such as paintballing or go-karting. This type of activity can help to 'socialize' the team but should not be confused with professionally organized and facilitated programmes for maximizing the input of the team in resolving potential conflict and mitigating project risk.

CDM rightly stresses the importance of:

Communication - Co-operation - Co-ordination

and this is unlikely to evolve naturally. The complex nature of construction projects leads to teams that tend to coalesce slowly and resolve conflict – whether it be technical, commercial or personal- on a trial and error basis.

So how do successful project teams differ from the average?

1. They are united in their desire to deliver a successful project outcome and are proud to be associated with the enterprise. (eg. Channel Tunnel Rail Link, London Eye)

2. The team is made up of people who have confidence in their own ability to carry out their allotted role, and are confident that the team as a whole knows what it is doing.

3. There is a culture of openness, respect and trust between team members which makes risk management and problem solving a creative, collaborative process rather than the individual responsibility of one team member ('its your problem').

4. The team recognizes that individuals have more to offer than merely in their specialist area of knowledge or expertise, but can contribute on a variety of aspects of the project, given the opportunity. This is particularly true when buildability and hazard elimination considerations are being discussed.

5. Production activity is efficient with the flow of design and other relevant information being generated in a timely fashion, allowing proper planning and risk management of the work to be carried out - before production starts. Late design changes are recognized as increasing both commercial and health and safety risk.

6. There is a strong sense of cohesion and team spirit. The team recognizes that they succeed or fail as one – there are no factions.

THINK POINT:
What do you do to **build the team** for your projects?

THE CLIENT LEADS THE TEAM

Many clients, particularly those who do not procure construction projects on a regular basis, overestimate the abilities of the designers and contractors they employ to collaborate, communicate and work effectively as a team. This is as true for a domestic client having a kitchen extension or loft conversion, as it is for a property developer, utilities company or public body procuring building or infrastructure works.

> Richard was a successful entrepreneur who through purchasing a scaffolding business, acquired ownership of a riverside site with the potential to be developed for residential use. As he had no previous project experience, his financial advisers proposed that the architect who had carried out the original planning submission be appointed to both lead the design team and project manage the development of two blocks containing 24 apartments valued at £2 million.
>
> Richard quickly realised that the architect's expectation of how they discharged their duties was very different from his own. He became increasingly frustrated at the lack of planning and poor communication exhibited by the designers and contractors.
>
> Despite having no previous construction experience, Richard did recognise that a successful project depends on the commitment of the people doing the work, and effective co-ordination of their various activities.
>
> He took it upon himself to get involved in the site supervision of the sub-contractors. He got to know the supervisors personally, showed them what the finished job would look like and explained the standard of work he expected. He used weekly meetings on Monday mornings to ensure that everyone was clear what the site goals were, and to resolve any issues relating to design or specification which had arisen since the last discussion.

A lack of leadership from the client can often be because the client simply doesn't know what to do, or how to do it. Although the appointment of a CDM co-ordinator is only a legal requirement for notifiable projects, every project, whatever its size or nature, would benefit from someone carrying out the role of advising the Client on how to ensure the project is delivered safely and with minimal risk for the end user.

There appears to be a general lack of understanding throughout the Industry as to the full scope of the CDM co-ordinator role and how it can best be employed to benefit everyone involved with the project, from the Client to the operatives who will work on the construction and maintenance of the facility.

The key to any management system is to establish clearly defined processes that everyone can understand and follow. The process for managing the design risks associated with a construction project can be divided into distinct phases:-

Phase 1   The Pre-construction Phase. (*Building the Team*)
               - from project inception to the appointment of the Principal
               Contractor

Phase 2   The Construction Phase (*Building the Facility*)
               - from the commencement of construction activities on site
               (including site investigation, demolition and enabling works)
               up to the point that the owner/occupier takes over operation
               of the facility.

Phase 3   The Post-construction Phase. (*Building the Business*)
               - from the point where the facility goes 'live' to the end of its
               operational life.

Phase 4   The Demolition Phase (*End of the Business*)

Before looking at each of these phases in detail, it is important to appreciate the nature and significance of business processes. Processes comprise a sequence of clearly defined steps or activities that if followed consistently, dramatically increase the likelihood that the desired outcomes will be achieved. Whilst processes (unlike procedures) contain a degree of flexibility that allows for differing sets of circumstances, there is a clear appreciation that failure to carry out all the steps, in the correct sequence, will increase the risk of failure or at least a reduction in the quality of the process results.

PHASE 1: BUILDING THE TEAM

Irrespective of whether the Client operates in the Public, Private or Third sector, their focus at the outset of the project will be on getting the best return on their capital investment.

There are many factors that a client will have to contend with in the early stages of a new project; the involvement of the CDM co-ordinator is critical during this period. Failure to make an early appointment will lead to decisions being made without fully exploring the implications. The first task a CDM co-ordinator must carry out is to ensure that the Client appreciates that their actions, at the start of the process, will have a major bearing on the performance of the project team and the results they deliver on the Client's behalf.

Many clients, understandably, make the mistake of assuming that because the advisers, designers and contractors they have appointed have previously worked on similar projects (in some cases as members of the same team), they will naturally form an effective and efficient team, committed to delivering the project goals with little input from the Client.

The evidence from numerous projects is that, in reality, the Client is hiring a number of 'specialists' - construction professionals who have considerable knowledge and skills relating to some aspects of the construction process, but often with little or no knowledge of others, and little appreciation of the roles and expertise of other members of the team.

It is also true that the acquisition of technical expertise does not necessarily translate into the ability to communicate either easily or effectively with other members of the team. Many construction professionals develop a defensive attitude to discussing aspects of the project for which they either:

a] consider to be their sole responsibility e.g. technical issues
or
b] do not consider their responsibility e.g. health & safety issues

How the Client and CDM co-ordinator address this issue depends at what point the CDM co-ordinator appointment is made.

The ACOP states

"Early appointment of the CDM co-ordinator is crucial for effective planning and establishing management arrangements from the start. The Regulations require the appointment to take place as soon as is practical after initial design work or other preparation for construction work has begun. This allows the client to appraise their project needs and objectives, including the business case and any possible constraints on development to enable them to decide whether or not to proceed with the project before appointing the

CDM co-ordinator. The CDM co-ordinator needs to be in a position to be able to co-ordinate health and safety aspects of the design work and advise on the suitability and compatibility of designs, and therefore they <u>*should be appointed before significant detailed design work begins.*</u>''

For a client to gain the most benefit from the CDM process, ideally, a capable CDM co-ordinator should be the first appointment made. However, in reality, professional and technical advisers, lead (and other) designers may well have been involved prior to the formal appointment of a CDM co-ordinator. It is quite likely that these appointments will have been made without a rigorous assessment of the competence of the people involved to fulfil their health and safety responsibilities. It is worth noting that until a formal CDM-co-ordinator (CDM-c) appointment is made the Client will be considered as holding these duties.

Although there is naturally a great deal of attention paid to assessing the health and safety competence of contractors, the design risk management process requires all members of the team to be knowledgeable and motivated to eliminate hazards and reduce risks at an early stage in the development of the project. Whilst assessing organizational competence is a useful first step, ultimately it is the knowledge and commitment of those individuals who make up the project team which will lead to a successful project. It is imperative that the Client 'buys in' to this approach as only they can insist that those already appointed commit to the team integration process.

The amount of effort required, and the approach used to gain full understanding and co-operation will vary from project to project. In many cases, an initial project risk review meeting, chaired by the Client and facilitated by the CDM co-ordinator will be an effective way of uniting the team.

The Prevention of Human Misery

One of the essential requirements for any construction professional to contribute to design risk management is an appreciation of 'The Causes of Human Misery'. Fortunately, many in the project team will have little or no personal experience of the consequences of a workplace accident. Depending on the level of previous training, participants in such a workshop may or may not be able to identify the primary causes of deaths and serious injuries on UK construction sites over recent years. For the design risk assessment process to be effective it is important to appreciate that the major causes of serious injuries and death are largely the same from year to year.

Without fail the number one cause of serious injury in Construction (and elsewhere) is:-

Falls from height

Despite more attention being paid to the prevention of falls on construction sites in recent years, around 30% of all serious incidents causing death or permanent injury are as a result of falling. Whilst many of the victims contributed to their own accidents by adopting unsafe methods of working, the law now views those who designed or planned the work as having a responsibility for considering how the risk of falls might be mitigated. Whether a different approach could eliminate the need to work at height, or at least reduce the amount of exposure to 'at height' working should at least be considered.

As many serious injuries result from falls of under two metres, this issue requires careful consideration not only when designing major structural elements but also many of the internal/fit-out activities involving dry-lining, electrical, mechanical and painting trades who have traditionally worked from step ladders, trestles and other unsuitable access equipment. Likewise, the cleaning and maintenance of structures and building services can expose workers to the risk of falling. Decisions taken early in the project can deliver dramatic benefits both in terms of worker safety and reduced maintenance costs, or create difficulties for facility managers and their teams, for the whole life of the facility.

Other regular causes of serious injuries and sometimes fatalities include

- Falling Objects
- Collapsing or overturning structures
- Contact with electricity
- Contact with moving plant and vehicles

A large government building in Wales was designed with a foundation detail involving an inner reinforced concrete wall and an outer wall constructed from blockwork. The two leaves of the wall were to be tied together using rigid steel ties and the cavity between the two filled with concrete. The average height (depth) of the foundation walling was approximately 1 metre, but in the section around the lift shaft base this increased to almost 2 metres.

The block walling construction and cavity filling operation had been progressing for some weeks without incident when, as the deeper section was being cavity filled, the blockwork 'blew' under pressure from the wet concrete being poured into the cavity. A worker supervising the filling operation from a ladder leaning against the block wall was thrown backwards as the blockwork burst and collapsed. He fell and suffered fatal injuries when his head hit a concrete block lying on the ground in the area where he landed..

The Principal Contractor was prosecuted and fined £200,000 with costs of over £70,000. The judge said the impact on the dead man's family 'can hardly be imagined.'

Whilst many factors contributed to the incident and its fatal consequences, the foundation design, as it evolved, appears to have been chosen without recognition of the potential problems such a construction detail could generate. Although the hazards associated with working at height and the pressure exerted by liquid concrete were well understood by the Principal Contractor, the communication process with the sub-contract workers carrying out this operation failed to convey the necessity of following the intended safe method of working which, if adhered to, would have mitigated these hazards.

Even when an accident does not result in a fatality the consequences for many of those seriously injured in accidents on construction sites are catastrophic-

- Physical disability
- Loss of livelihood or restricted work opportunities
- Long term health problems
- Significant financial loss
- Emotional and psychological problems
- Domestic upheaval
- Premature death

Whilst the impact on victims and their families is dramatic, the industry in general is largely unaware of these consequences as site accidents are often quickly forgotten.

In addition to the thousands of construction workers (as well as hundreds of members of the public) affected by accidents every year, tens of thousands of workers suffer long term damage to their health with similar consequences, as a result of exposure to harmful substances or unhealthy working environments.

The most common causes of premature death, ill health and reduced quality of life include:-

- Exposure to asbestos
- Exposure to harmful chemicals (e.g. Paints, solvents, coatings etc)
- Exposure to excessive vibration
- Exposure to excessive noise

Whereas these might previously have been considered as 'site issues', to be managed by the contractors, CDM places a clear duty on those who design, specify or plan the works to consider whether the chosen solution increases the workers' exposure to harmful substances or working environments.

Without a personal appreciation of the causes of 'Human Misery' associated with life-changing accidents or contracting a debilitating condition such as vibration white finger, the project team is unlikely to give proper consideration to these issues.

The Risk Management Model
There is little doubt that construction professionals, for a variety of reasons, feel more pressured in the current business environment than ever before, with stress-related health problems increasingly appearing as a cause of staff absence in construction organizations. The reasons for this trend are numerous, but fundamentally revolve around the fact that the construction process involves reconciling two fundamentally different management demands:-

- *Production* demands - getting the job done!
- *Compliance* demands - doing the job right!

Production demands are <u>internally</u> imposed:-

- Delivery of the facility to a timescale and in a sequence determined by the Client/Operator
- Completion of the facility within an agreed budget
- Incorporation of materials and components to a specified standard

Compliance demands are <u>externally</u> imposed:-

- Criminal and civil obligations in relation to the health, safety and welfare of the workforce together with others affected by the project
- Legislation relating to protection of the natural and built environments
- Regulatory standards relating to the performance of the facility e.g. Planning consents, building regulations, quality standards

The project team is likely to be more aware of the internal requirements which are generally stated explicitly whereas the external drivers may be largely invisible to many in the project team. The twin pressures of **Cost** and **Time** whether explicitly expressed or not can exert a vice-like grip on the thinking of designers and contractors alike For this reason they could be viewed as the 'Primary Drivers', dominating the discussions and decisions made as the project progresses. The Compliance aspects of the project could therefore be viewed as 'Secondary Drivers', but as they are generally legally enforceable, they should be viewed as 'Mandatory Drivers' - and clients and their project teams disregard them at their peril.

The design risk management process requires that the members of the project team understand that the Primary and Mandatory Drivers have to be considered as equally important and that an iterative approach, where each option is assessed against all the criteria, is necessary to arrive at a decision which, on balance, best satisfies all requirements.

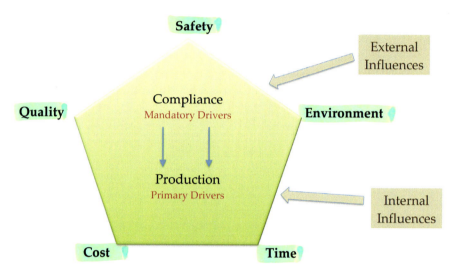

FIG 6: THE 'PENTAGON' RISK MANAGEMENT MODEL

For example, where, owing to poor ground conditions a structure requires a piled foundation solution, there will often be a variety of options to choose from such as bored cast in-situ, CFA, driven pre-cast concrete or tubular steel etc.

Each solution will have particular technical, cost and time implications and these may well determine which option is selected, without giving due regard to health, safety or environmental considerations.

Driven piles will tend to be quicker to install but are likely to induce significant noise and vibration, potentially creating problems to on site workers as well as neighbours and adjacent structures.

Cast in-situ piles may produce lower levels of noise and vibration but may involve manual handling of reinforcement cages, handling and disposal of wet concrete and the use of vibrating hand tools to trim the pile heads.

If the ground is heavily contaminated the potential health and environmental hazards associated with toxic pile arisings will need to be considered, as well as pollution of surface and ground water resources.

Every structure on every site will represent a unique combination of issues for consideration. A very effective way to evaluate the risks and select the 'best fit' option is to review the design proposals as a team. Whilst the designer of the piling will have considered many of the issues already, a design review will allow other members of the team to contribute by asking questions and perhaps supplying additional information not previously known to the designer. This approach would certainly support the argument that a 'suitable and sufficient' risk assessment had taken place.

A project review meeting held when the design of key elements of the project had begun but were not so far advanced that other options could not be considered, would enable each activity involving significant hazards to be considered in turn. The decisions taken could be recorded and communicated to the Principal Contractor as part of the pre-construction information.

Selecting a competent Principal Contractor
The appointment of a competent Principal Contractor is clearly a critical step in delivering a safe project. The timing of their appointment will owe much to the procurement method chosen by the client (and their advisers.)

The Regulations state that the principal contractor should be appointed

'as soon as the Client knows enough about the project to select a suitable contractor.'

and emphasizes the importance of early appointment to allow

'the principal contractor and other specialists, for example maintenance contractors and facilities management experts, to make a substantial contribution to ensuring the buildability and maintainability of the structure under construction.'

Although the ACOP sets out core criteria for assessing the competence of contractors it fails to address the **process** by which a client and their advisers can satisfy themselves that the construction works will be carried out by a proficient, safety conscious team.

Assuming that the core project team has held a risk review workshop, the members will have developed an understanding of the significant residual risks (i.e. those that cannot be eliminated at the design stage). This information will be helpful in selecting a shortlist of contractors with the appropriate experience who may be invited to bid for the contract.

Within the bid documentation, (invitation to tender), there should be a summary of these significant residual risks with a requirement for the contractors to submit, as part of their bids, a broad indication of how they would propose to mitigate or control them.

Post-tender evaluation meetings naturally focus on financial issues. They should also include consideration of the contractors' proposals for managing the significant risk issues and should establish what allowances have been made within their price for the cost of mitigation measures.

It is not acceptable to separate the safety issues from the financial evaluation process - although it is extremely common,. All aspects of the project are inextricably linked. Contractors who have addressed the identified risk issues at the tender stage and priced appropriate mitigation measures accordingly are more likely to deliver a satisfactory performance than those who treat safety as a secondary issue to be dealt with further down the line.

Meetings with prospective principal contractors should involve those managers who will be directly responsible for the construction phase (e.g. Project manager, construction manager, etc.) They should be able to elaborate on the safe systems of work outlined in their company's tender proposal and answer questions from other members of the project team.

This approach not only allows the Client (whose duty it is to assess the competence of their appointees), the opportunity to gain a better understanding of each contractor's proposals, but also enables them to judge the character and professionalism of those whom they must entrust to lead the most hazardous phase of the project.

The selection and appointment of a Principal Contractor will be based on a variety of considerations, not least cost. An often overlooked fact is that the outturn cost of a project will often be considerably higher than the bid price accepted by the Client at the appointment stage. Whatever the contractual arrangements, the best way of managing variations in scope, overcoming technical problems and dealing with the many unforeseen developments that can beset even well run projects, is as a united team.

If a Client has confidence in the project team, and if the members of that team feel they will be fairly treated, there is a better chance that when conflicts arise, they will be fully discussed and resolved with due regard for health and safety as well as time and cost considerations.

Unfortunately, it is often the case that the appointment of contractors is made without engaging with the 'works team' before construction activity gets underway.

Construction projects, by their nature, require a great deal of conflict resolution - that is, addressing conflicting priorities, needs and wants in order to achieve the project goals. Is it not better to discuss in advance, how we will behave as a group, when such situations arise? If the Client (or any other team member) intends to 'point the finger' and duck their own responsibility when problems arise is it not better to establish this at the outset?

Alternatively, if the Client expects the team to pull together, use their collective expertise to best effect and is willing to accept that there may be some additional costs to be reimbursed in resolving such conflicts, this should also be stated at the outset.

A Client who wishes to meet with contractors' proposed key site personnel prior to appointment must be insistent from the outset, that this requirement will form a key part of the assessment process. They should not be thwarted by contractors with statements like:

'We don't know who will be available when the project starts'
 Or
'We can't guarantee that the people who attend the meeting will be the ones doing the job.'

THINK POINT:
However impressive a company's management system, or safety record, the truth is that their performance on the next project will largely be a function of the skills, experience and attitude of the individuals in the site team.

Investing a little time at the outset to get the right people 'on board' can deliver both tangible and intangible benefits.

Under CDM 2007 the Client is duty bound to assess the competence of those they appoint. This approach addresses competence at the personal rather than simply at the organizational level and allows a proper integration of the design and construction elements of the team.

PHASE 2 – BUILDING THE FACILITY
Selecting the Principal Contractor (PC) who best meets the needs of the project allows the Core Team to benefit from the PCs practical knowledge and experience to enhance the design risk review process.

At the earliest opportunity a buildability review involving the Core Team, Principal Contractor, key suppliers and contractors with design responsibility should be held to further refine the risk review process that began at the integration workshop.

Continuity is a key feature of an effective risk management process, so the individuals from the core team should resist the temptation to absent themselves from the 'Buildability' Review on the basis that;

'I have done my bit - let's leave it to the experts',
Or
'I have more important things to do.'

There is a huge benefit in different members of the team sharing what they know about how the project has developed, as well as their previous experiences of good and poor practice which may help the team to do things better this time around.

There is a great tendency for project meetings to focus on the technical issues with very little, if any, consideration being given to the organizational or 'people' issues. As part of the 'Integration' and 'Buildability' meetings, the team must consider two questions:-

1. What are the significant messages that we will need to communicate to the wider project workforce?
2. What means will we use to ensure that the messages are received and understood by everyone who will be part of the project, whatever the duration of their involvement?

THINK POINT:
How effective has communication been in projects you've worked on in the past?

What's in an induction?
The word 'induction' can be defined as:-

'the formal introduction or entry into an office or position.'

Over the last decade or so, a site induction has become a feature of most construction sites, with workers being required to attend some form of initial briefing, usually with a high 'safety' content, prior to being permitted to start work on site.

Depending on the nature of the project and the safety culture prevailing on site (driven either by the Client or the Principal Contractor), this induction may be no more than a short informal chat, or a lengthy formal session involving slide presentations, videos and safety lectures, sometimes lasting hours.

In the course of a year the average construction operative can expect to attend a number of such inductions. Although the content and duration of these inductions will vary considerably, they will generally have one thing in common:-

THEY WILL FAIL TO ENGAGE THE INDIVIDUAL WORKER IN ANY MEANINGFUL WAY WHATSOEVER.

The content of inductions typically revolves around site orientation and facilities, safety rules, procedures and the like. Delivery of these inductions is often by under-skilled and untrained presenters who may have to carry out the same task every morning of the week and can come to treat it as a routine chore.

Irrespective of the content and format, the message that the individual workers generally receive is:

"They don't care about me - they are just doing what they have to, to cover their own backs."

We once sat in on a site induction at a rail project in London. The forty five minute session was led by the resident safety manager who delivered a rapid fire PowerPoint presentation and concluded with asking attendees to complete a short questionnaire to demonstrate understanding. Apart from asking them which companies they worked for, he never engaged the (three) operatives present in any two-way communication whatsoever.

As you entered the site a large sign over the gate read:-

'WELCOME TO AN EXCELLENT PROJECT'

This slogan would have made a good starting point for engaging the workforce in a discussion about what makes for an excellent project, the kind of behaviour you could expect, etc., but perhaps the presenter thought that his presentation was already excellent.

The truth is he did not have any key messages for the workforce that would engage them in <u>wanting</u> to make a positive contribution to the success of the project. Instead he fell back on his knowledge of basic health and safety issues and believed that by simply telling them again what was expected, he was somehow influencing their behaviour.

It wasn't really his fault. He was simply repeating what happens on sites across the UK because no thought had been given by the project team to our two questions:-

1. What are the significant messages.....?
Whatever the project, one message should be communicated above all others if there is to be any positive engagement with the workforce:-

> 'We care about you and we don't want you to suffer harm or ill-health in any way, as a result of carrying out your duties in delivering this project.'

For the message to be meaningful, it has got to be endorsed by the Client and supported by their actions in dealing with the Core Project team and Principal Contractor. Without consistency of action the message will quickly become an empty slogan which will help to create a negative, rather than a positive safety culture.

If this were to be the starting point for site inductions, the next logical step would be to engage the workers in understanding the nature of work to be carried out and the measures that would need to be adhered to, if the project is to avoid the creation of human misery.

It is quite common for the workforce to be viewed as an unreliable, ignorant and potentially troublesome element who will deliberately flout the site rules given half a chance. Whilst it is true that many of the workforce will lack the academic education of the professional members of the team, this should not detract from the view that the workers can make a vital contribution to maintaining a safe and productive site, once properly engaged.

2. What means will we use to ensure the messages are received and understood?
Having a clear message to communicate is the first requirement. It may take some time for the project team to formulate an agreed message in terms that can be readily imparted to others. It has to be a message that individuals feel personally committed to, and can explain in plain language to others.

For example:-

> 'Every project decision will take into account the health and safety implications for those affected by that decision.'

This message would apply equally to client, designers, contractors and the individual workers going about their normal duties.

Currently, there is an over reliance on written communications – policy statements, risk assessments, safety rules, method statements, documented work procedures and the like - as if construction workers have to be 'told' how to work safely.

This approach disregards the simple fact that many of us don't like reading very much and may only take in a small amount of written information before becoming distracted. For all of its good intentions most of the paper produced for health and safety purposes is written without any real regard for the current level of understanding of the intended audience.

THINK POINT:
Recent research in the US identified that whereas the reading age of the average construction worker was equivalent to a ten year-old, safety literature was written by people with an average reading age of eighteen.

Whilst the volume of safety material produced has multiplied exponentially over the last decade, the average construction (not to mention health and safety) professional has probably done very little to improve the effectiveness of either their written or other communication skills.

We are convinced that there are substantial improvements to be gained, for the Client, the Project team and individual workers if a more 'people-centred' approach were taken to project risk management, with less emphasis on paper and more on engaging all participants in developing sound working methods.

PHASE 3 – BUILDING THE BUSINESS

The Construction Industry is a service industry. It exists to supply clients in the public and private sectors with the facilities they need to carry out their core business or operational activities. Clients in general have little interest in, or understanding of, the construction process; the project is no more than a necessary step in translating their vision into reality.

Many construction professionals view the project as an end in itself and have little or no understanding of the client's long term goals or the critical aspects of the project delivery.

Put another way, whilst the client's main focus is on the point when they can start to integrate the facility into their business operations, this is precisely the point at which the industry thinks that the job is almost done and starts to lose interest.

This period in the project's life is probably the most frustrating and aggravating for all concerned. The ritual of preparing and dealing with 'snagging lists' is a testament to the industry's poor attitude to customer service and for the client represents a period of disruption to their business operation that can last for months or years. The CDM 07 ACOP quotes a report of the Royal Academy of Engineering titled 'The long term costs of owning and using buildings (1998). The main thrust of the report is that construction professionals need to understand how the performance of the facility, as designed and built, will impact over the long term on the productivity and operating costs of their enterprise. As an illustration the report states that in the case of a commercial client's office building, for every £1 the client invests in construction, they will typically spend £5 on maintenance and will incur operating costs (i.e. the costs associated with their core business) of £200.

> Typical operating and owning costs for an office building are in the ratio:
>
> - 1 for construction costs
> - 5 for maintenance costs
> - 200 for business operating costs
>
> Report of the Royal Academy of Engineering -*The Long Term Cost of Owning & Using Buildings (1999)*

The report suggests that similar ratios may apply to other types of facilities. If this point was clearly understood by clients, designers and contractors it would help them to shift the focus from short term cost driven considerations, to operability and maintainability issues, with safety and long term considerations being given greater attention.

In Stephen Covey's book 'The Seven Habits of Highly Effective People', habit number two is:

'Begin with the end in mind.'

Owing to the fragmented nature of the delivery team, and the pressure of short term demands, combined with a lack of awareness of whole life costs and operational productivity, many issues are decided without any appreciation of the long term implications - financial or human.

Although perhaps not stated explicitly in the legislation, for CDM to be effective, it is clearly necessary for the project team to spend some time in the early stages of the job, gaining an understanding of the Client's business drivers, and the functional (and other) requirements they are looking for the facility to fulfil.

Clients often do not have a fully developed view of what they require at the outset of a project; many of the problems encountered during construction projects stem from the clients belief that they can continually change their mind on design or specification issues without it impacting on the team performance and consequently the progress of the job.

Many construction professionals lack the ability to establish a clear and comprehensive brief with the Client at the outset.

As a minimum, the principle should be established at the outset of every project that late design changes have health and safety as well as production implications ; they should be viewed as events that are likely to increase risk so should therefore be carefully thought through before proceeding.

If CDM was functioning as originally intended, one of the major beneficiaries would be the organization responsible for operating, maintaining and cleaning the facility. Some Clients will have their own teams but many major organizations now contract the work to Facilities Management (FM) companies who will provide personnel and sub-contractors to carry out a range of functions that may include cleaning, catering, general and specialist maintenance and security functions - freeing up the client's management to focus on their core 'business'. Conversations with many FM managers have provided a picture of an industry that is generally failing to address the health and safety of those that will be exposed to risk during the life of the building.

Lack of safe systems to access, clean and maintain facades and roof areas is a recurring theme.

An FM manager at a hospital in the South of England described how the building (which was less than ten years old) contained a number of enclosed, glazed courtyards. Whenever work was required to the internal facades scaffolding (for the access towers) had to be brought through the building. Because the façade had been designed without anchorage points to tie-in the tower, all four sides of the courtyard had to be scaffolded, to provide stability to the section being worked on.

The only access to these courtyards was via the main hospital routes, requiring large quantities of scaffold tube, boards and fittings to be transported, by hand through live corridors.

The Construction Industry does not have a monopoly on poor communication and weak management. However, the complex nature of the undertaking demands that clients and their teams recognize the need to develop open and effective means of interacting so that projects are delivered without repeating the mistakes that recur time and again, costing time, money and above all, human misery.

What the law demands through the CDM Regulations and associated legislation is really only what one might expect from any team that considers itself to be professional. The industry is full of hardworking, diligent and capable individuals who want to do the right thing.

Unfortunately in many cases:

the whole is **less** than the sum of the parts.

SECTION 3 REVIEW

- High-performing Construction teams can be created if effort is directed to the right things.

- In successful projects the Client leads the team and sets the culture under which the project will operate.

- Build the team first – and then build the project

- Focus more on people and less on paperwork.

- Be clear about the messages you are communicating to the team.

SECTION 4

BACK TO
THE FUTURE

WHERE WE CONSIDER:

Are we making progress?

The benefits of new technologies

The obsession with paperwork

'We shall never cease from striving, and the end of all our striving will be to arrive where we began, and to know the place for the first time.'

MAKING PROGRESS?

Perhaps the most difficult aspect of improving performance, whether as an individual, an organisation or an industry, is being able to gauge, over time, how much progress has been made and how much scope there is to improve further.

The Latham Report 'Constructing the Team' (1994) and Egan Report 'Rethinking Construction' (1998) acted as catalysts in addressing some of the endemic problems which had dogged the UK Construction Industry in the preceding decades.

From the late 1990s up to the global recession of 2007-2009 the industry did change in a number of significant ways:-

- A culture of sharing best practice began to develop amongst the major players
- A massive increase in the use of information technology (IT) led to ever faster communication of ideas, information and data.
- Health and Safety legislation demanded a more formal approach to managing risk in the workplace leading to a huge growth in safety driven bureaucracy.
- An increasing reliance on private finance to fund the construction of state-sponsored infrastructure and facilities ushered in new forms of procurement and contractual relationships.

If the first decade of the new millennium was characterised by a construction boom funded by cheap money, the next is likely to see the emphasis on curtailed spending as both public and private sector clients demand 'a lot more for a lot less.'

2009 was the year when major UK construction clients, including Network Rail, BAA and the privatised water companies began to review their approach to procurement, with, in some cases, the apparent intent of moving away from 'cosy' partnering arrangements. One director with responsibility for capital programmes said at the time 'I am not throwing out framework procurement but I am approaching it in a very different way. Competition is the best way for me to demonstrate value for money to the regulators.'

Other major clients, particularly in the retail sector, were more robust in their approach, asking their framework consultants and contractors to accept cost reduction targets of 20% or more if they wished to be involved in future projects. The temptation to procure construction services on the basis of 'lowest cost wins' is understandable when budgets are squeezed and. the industry is short of work. However, those with long memories of how the industry operated 'pre – Latham' may feel a little queasy at the prospect of returning to the era of bidding low and hoping to make up the deficit by pursuing claims for every change and variation.

Historically, the industry has, with some honourable exceptions, shown little enthusiasm for analysing the out-turn performance of completed projects. Many in the industry refuse to acknowledge that the initial bid cost may bear little resemblance to the out-turn cost, if risk has not been clearly identified and allocated to the party best placed to mitigate it. Likewise, completion delays and protracted snagging periods are considered as normal to most construction professionals, however costly and aggravating they may be to the client. Too often, by the time the project is complete and the final picture is clear, most of the project team has moved on to new projects, potentially to make the same mistakes for a different client in a different setting.

FROM EGAN TO WOLSTENHOLME

In late 2009 a report entitled 'Never Waste a Good Crisis' was published by Constructing Excellence which gives a useful overview of how much progress the Industry has made in the decade or so since the Egan Report was published. In the forward to the report Sir John Egan sums up the limited progress achieved to date:-

> *'Since 1998 we could have had a revolution and what we have achieved is a bit of an improvement.'*

The Chair of the Review Team was Andrew Wolstenholme. The Executive Summary of the report enlarged on Sir John's assessment:-

> *Since Sir John's Task Force published its report 'Rethinking Construction' in 1998, there has been some progress but nowhere near enough. Few of the Egan Targets have been met in full, while most have fallen considerably short. Where improvements have been achieved, too often the commitment to Egan's principles has been skin deep. In some sectors, such as housing, construction simply does not matter, because there is such a limited understanding of how value can be created through the construction process.'*

It is worth reminding ourselves of the five key drivers identified by the Egan Task Force as being central to bringing about wholesale change in Construction:-

1. *Committed Leadership* – management believing in and being totally committed to performance improvement

2. *Focus on the Customer* – providing a product that the customer wants, when they want it, and at a price that reflects its value.

3. *Integrated Processes and Teams* – delivering value to the customer efficiently and eliminating waste.

4. *A Quality-Driven Agenda* – getting it right first time, with zero defects, on time and on budget.

5 *Commitment to People* – a commitment to Health & Safety and training and development of staff. A 'no-blame' culture based on mutual interdependence and trust.

The Task Force set targets for the Industry to improve performance, based on experience from leading clients and contractors in the UK and overseas, such as 10% annual reductions in capital costs and construction time, and 20% annual reductions in defects and accidents.

It is questionable whether this rather simplistic approach to target setting is helpful in bringing about cultural change but at least it gave the Industry (or at least those parts that were interested) some concept of performance indicators. The Team called on construction clients to show leadership and put forward 'demonstration projects' to show the benefits of implementing the reports recommendations.

The Wolstenholme Report based its assessment, to a significant degree, on the body of evidence generated by the five hundred or so demonstration projects that were completed during the Egan decade. Although these projects consistently showed superior performance relative to the rest of the Construction sector the report highlights the cultural shortcomings that existed even here:-

'The problem, however, as our survey reveals, is that even where the principles of Rethinking Construction *have been adopted, too often the commitment is skin deep. Scratch beneath the surface and you find many so called partners still seek to avoid or exploit risk to maximise their own profits, rather than find ways to share risk and collaborate genuinely so that all can profit.'*

In canvassing the views of nearly one thousand construction professionals, the report reveals a picture of some excellent examples of good practice **'against a backdrop of fairly entrenched behaviour.'** One respondent referred to the **'minority club '**that had adopted the Egan philosophy whilst another commented **'There is no evidence that the progress made in a small percentage of the industry's activities will ever spread to the rest.'**

Other views expressed suggest there is a concern about the quality of training available in the Industry from providers **'who have jumped on the bandwagon.'** Perhaps surprisingly, only just over half of the respondents considered integrating the process and the team around the product as being very important.

Looking ahead to the next ten years, respondents were clear about where the industry needed to focus its attention – people issues. Topics such as *'Training'*, *'Skills development'*, *'People management'* and *'The constitution of the labour force and its regulation '* were all frequently cited.

From the survey the report concludes:-

> *'It is clear that the stated aim of genuinely embedding the spirit of change has not been met. There is not enough evidence of a united resolve across the diverse constituencies of UK Construction to achieve Egan's vision of a modern construction industry.*

From the human behaviour perspective it is obvious that the private sector, which accounts for approximately 60% of total construction demand, is primarily 'profit driven.' This often leads to 'short-term' thinking and an inability to recognise the value of investing time and money upfront to identify solutions that will deliver long-term benefits to the client. It might be expected that the public sector would be more receptive to the concept of collaborative working to deliver best value solutions. Whilst there are examples both in the public and private sectors of strong clients promoting a collaborative culture amongst its project teams they are still the exception rather than the rule

> Founded by Birmingham City Council, the Birmingham Construction Partnership was a unique collaboration of contractors, design and specialist supply chains set up to deliver all capital projects with a budget above £100k. With a true partnering approach, the team were able to align all construction projects to the City's corporate objectives of sustainability, whole life costing, best value, local employment, training and strategic alliances. After one year, the Partnership achieved a 52% improvement in projects delivered to time and a 29% improvement in projects delivered to budget.

In the absence of such leadership, many construction professionals will default to the traditional approach of 'playing their cards close to their chest' and 'only doing what we are being paid for.'

The Welsh Water Capital Alliance was a strategic partnering team set up to deliver around 60% of Welsh Water's capital investment programme during 2000-2005. It comprised Dwr Cymru Welsh Water, United Utilities, six strategic design/construction partners and a number of specialist roles. The partners committed to work collaboratively in order to meet the needs of the Alliance. Welsh Water succeeded in reducing its cost base by 60% and was assessed by OFWAT (the water industry regulator) as having the best overall performance in the sector.

USING AND ABUSING INFORMATION TECHNOLOGY (IT)

If the historic problems of the construction industry have been rooted in its highly fragmented nature, the growth of IT and its many applications could be viewed as a potentially powerful force for enabling the efficient management of project information and enhanced communication between the members of the project team.

Perhaps the two most significant developments over the last 10-15 years have been the use of Collaborative Extranets and 3D modelling software.

Collaborative Extranets
Project extranets represent probably the most successful application of IT, in terms of the benefits for construction projects, in the last decade. By harnessing the power of the Internet, these systems allow users to share drawings, specifications, schedules, programmes and every other type of electronic document, generated as part of the project process.

Even projects of a modest scale need to deal with increasing volumes of documentation and the contributors and users of this information will typically be dispersed in offices in different parts of the country and often many miles from the site of construction. From their beginnings as a document management system, the most advanced project extranets will have the following features:

- Drawing issue and document control
- On-line viewing and mark-up
- Approvals/workflow
- Discussion tools
- Reporting facilities
- Package management
- Contact management

In addition, the system provides a robust audit trail and efficient project archiving facilities.

The benefits of using the integration and communication potential of IT in this way can be considerable:-

- Substantial reductions in the time taken for drawings and other project documents to get from 'the drawing board' to the intended recipients.
- Control over the use of superseded drawings and revised documents
- Systematic allocation of access rights to ensure the right people get the right level of information at the right time
- Big reductions in the amount of paper printed
- Project information can be accessed from anywhere in the world
- The opportunity for project partners to review and comment on design development on-line
- Dramatic reductions in time spent tracking, logging and filing project correspondence and documents.

Whilst not easy to quantify, the cost and time benefits accruing from the use of project extranets must be considerable particularly on large and complex projects such as the schools and hospital schemes delivered under the PFI /PPP model, which have proliferated over the last decade.

Just as importantly, the project extranet helps to promote a 'one team culture' by defining who is in the team and setting out protocols for communication. However, on its own, it will not create the sense of purpose and shared interest which are key to delivering the best project performance.

Building Information Modelling (BIM)

By comparison, the use of computer generated 3D models of construction projects, building on the development of CAD 2D graphics, has been surprisingly slow. The first 3D modelling software (such as Archicad) was being used by progressive UK construction companies as long ago as the mid 1990's. Although only able to produce very basic models compared with current software, they represented a step change in the way members of a project team were able to understand and appreciate what was being proposed by the designers.

Although construction professionals have traditionally relied on 2D drawings to provide most of the information required to get the job built, many people, including experienced professionals, can find it difficult to quickly understand and assimilate the drawing information produced by other parties. 2D computer aided design (CAD) was well established by the time 3D modelling was developed, in what could be seen as a logical progression.

Subsequently, software developments have enabled 4D, 5D and even 6D models that not only define the physical features of a project but also cost, sequencing and sustainability information relating to the elements that make up the project.

Initially 3D modelling was used to produce 'fly-around' models that gave the uninitiated an overview of what the development or project would look like. Though fairly crude in terms of technology and detail, these models represented a significant step forward in the team's ability to communicate what the project was about, and did not require the viewer to have any particular knowledge or experience in order to engage with the project team.

As with all things IT, the functionality (capability) of the modelling software increased at a more rapid rate than the ability of the industry to use what was currently available. A recent survey in America suggested that very few organisations have made the transition to 3D based design.

Catalyst's Robert Green surveyed over 600 CAD managers with the following results:-

- 19% of respondents still worked totally in 2D
- 51% of respondents worked in 2D but were 'evaluating' 3D
- 24% used a combination of 2D and 3D
- 6% of respondents had made the full transition to 3D

The survey was in line with a previous survey of American business owners which showed that about 30% had tried BIM on one or more projects.

The picture in the UK is less clear but we can be fairly sure that the move towards BIM is lagging behind the US by a considerable distance. Whilst modelling has been used quite widely for steelwork design and clash detection, there are few clients like BAA who have embraced 3D modelling as a project wide tool. A recent survey by the National Building Specification found that only 13% of those working in the industry had heard of BIM.

Of course there are many reasons to explain the slow take-up of what is clearly a very useful technology – the up front investment both in time and money required, time pressures, a natural tendency to 'stick with what we know', and perhaps the desire on the part of some professionals to keep some mystique around their technical knowledge.

DOCUMENT PROLIFERATION

If the take up of BIM has been slow to develop, the adoption of the more mundane IT products has been much more comprehensive. It is easy to forget that until the late 1990s the use of Word documents, Excel spreadsheets and e-mail accounts was not widespread amongst construction professionals, particularly those working on site. For many of those working in the industry, having access to a PC or laptop is a development of the last decade or so.

Whilst the benefits of widespread use of IT are obvious - faster communication, instant transfer of project information between members of the project team etc. – it is debatable whether the overall impact of this development has been to increase or diminish effective communication and team working. In particular, the ease with which documents, forms and schedules can be produced and modified by individuals with no more than basic IT skills contrasts dramatically with the previous era when each document would have had to be drafted longhand by the construction professional and passed to a secretary or typist to produce the finished product. The typewriter ruled. The facility to 'cut and paste' from one document to another just did not exist.

The growth in IT-enabled construction professionals coincided with the growing demand for health and safety risk assessments, method statements and supporting documentation. Although the need to produce formal risk assessments had first arisen to satisfy the requirements of the Control of Substances Hazardous to Health (COSHH) regulations in the early 1990s, it appears that the exponential growth in health and safety risk management documentation only began after the revision of the Management of Health and Safety at Work Regulations in 1999.

The picture today is of an industry that demands often excessive quantities of paperwork, much of it standardised, to be produced and approved before even basic operations are permitted to be carried out, regardless of the competencies of those responsible for executing the work.

Although little research has been carried out to assess the impact of this change of emphasis (i.e. relying on paperwork to manage risk) on project performance, anecdotal evidence from across the industry suggests that increasing amounts of management time are spent on producing and reviewing this documentation. A common refrain is:

"Staff seem to spend all their time in front of a computer screen; they don't seem to get time to get out on to site to see what is happening."

From HSE statistics it can be seen that the decline in the number of reported three day lost time injuries in the Construction sector between 1998/99 and

2008/09 for employees was 9195 to 6789 a 27% reduction. For self-employed workers the figure rose from 381 to 562 – an increase of 47%.

For major injuries the figures are similar:

	1998/99	2008/09	Change
Employees	4289	3286	-24%
Self-employed	367	627	+70%

And for fatal injuries:

	1998/99	2008/09	Change
Employees	47	33	-30%
Self-employed	18	20	+11%

As we have said previously, it is unwise to draw too many conclusions from statistical data alone. Under-reporting of accidents is well recognised so the HSE figures can only paint a part of the picture. However, it would appear there has been some progress made in reducing the risk to construction workers over the last ten years.

The critical question has to be:-,

Considering the massive increase in time, effort, training and bureaucracy invested by (at least some) sectors of the Industry, are we getting a satisfactory return in terms of reduced physical and financial consequences?

Secondly:

If we are going to improve on the current performance – and there is clearly plenty of scope to do so – will this current approach deliver?

Once again we have to rely on anecdotal evidence but many construction professionals, particularly those working in high risk sectors such as energy and rail, would claim that an overly bureaucratic approach ultimately reduces effective communication and demotivates both managers and workers. This can lead to a culture where people fail to think for themselves and simply "carry out instructions" without necessarily understanding the potential risks or taking responsibility for how the work is done.

Just as importantly, a growing amount of management time is being absorbed by non-productive activities, in an attempt to satisfy perceived compliance requirements. As we saw in Section 2, production of excessive quantities of paperwork is not necessary to satisfy statutory obligations and is clearly at odds with the guiding principles of CDM 2007.

Not only is the obsession with paperwork largely unproductive, but the work patterns of construction professionals are gradually turning many of them from hands-on practitioners into over-critical permit-dispensers. Unless the Industry adopts a more people-centred approach to risk management it will become increasingly difficult to demonstrate that the team actually possesses the competencies to manage risk effectively and deliver a successful project.

SEVEN TRUTHS OF PROJECT RISK MANAGEMENT

In conclusion, it would seem that the industry needs to change its thinking if it is to achieve the kind of improvements that Egan and the 'minority club' have suggested are possible. We don't suggest that any change will happen quickly, but we do believe that those who sincerely wish to improve the experience of clients, professionals and workers consider the following:-

1. The client's approach is the key factor in the way the project is delivered.

2. CDM 2007 is a valuable aid for guiding clients (and others) in the ways of delivering successful projects.

3. If there were no legislation, the 'CDM Way' would still be the right way to manage risk and deliver successful projects.

4. The CDM Way – people matter more than paperwork

5. Paperwork is only an attempt at communication – what's the message?

6. The paperwork will only reduce when trust in the team increases.

7. Those with the greatest power are at least risk – those with the least power at greatest risk.

SECTION 5

SO WHAT SHOULD
WE BE DOING?

WHERE WE CONSIDER:

*How clients should
lead the project*

*What the co-ordination
role entails*

*The process for
managing design risk*

'If everyone is moving forward together,
then success takes care of itself.'

We will now consider the steps that any project team can take to fulfil the requirements of the CDM 2007 regulations in a way that brings benefits to the whole project team – and especially the client.

If the project is not notifiable to the HSE one or two of the following points may not be strictly necessary; however we would encourage the reader to apply the principles described here to their project to the extent that it will bring benefit to the team, irrespective of the strict legal requirements of the CDM Regulations.

THE CLIENT FUNCTION

If you are the client, you have a great opportunity to influence the way the project is delivered. Whilst domestic clients (i.e. householders having work done on their own home or the home of a family member that does not relate to a trade or business) are exempt from the legal duties imposed by CDM 2007, there are both moral and practical reasons why they, like other clients, should set the project team on the right course.

In many cases it will be obvious who is fulfilling the client role – as a rule of thumb, whoever initiates and funds the project activities is probably the client. However, there are many situations, both in the public and private sectors, where a number of parties may have a part to play in initiating and funding a project. In this situation it may be prudent for one party to elect, in writing, to accept the client duties under CDM 2007. In the absence of such a move, all parties will be deemed to hold these duties.

In the initial stages of the project, you should focus on the following:

1. Defining your expectations in terms of project delivery and health and safety performance
2. Selecting an individual or organisation to advise on managing project risk and CDM compliance
3. Assessing the competence of designers and contractors you appoint and taking steps to address any shortcomings, particularly in terms of health and safety, identified during the initial phase of the project.
4. Ensuring that information needed to permit the project team to develop 'safe' design solutions is made available, even if this means commissioning surveys (e.g. site investigations or asbestos surveys) to identify problem areas.

If you display contradictory attitudes towards managing risk this will communicate itself to the project team and undermine efforts to deliver a safe project. For example, imposing unrealistic timescales on project delivery or refusing to pay for adequate site investigation prior to developing the design will neutralise any stated intent to 'put health and safety first.'

Informed clients appreciate that the right action taken at the beginning of a project can save costly alterations further down the line and reduce the opportunities for accidents and health problems resulting from ill-thought out project decisions.

As a client you will not be held responsible for site accidents provided that you can demonstrate that you discharged your duties under CDM. If you can also show a genuine commitment to enhancing the welfare of the construction team then so much the better.

Case Study 1: London 2012 – the Way Forward

The Olympic Delivery Authority (ODA) was formally established on 1st April 2006 to deliver around £7 billion of major construction works on a largely derelict and polluted site in the eastern part of London to provide a theatre for the world's largest sporting event. From the outset this 'new' client recognised its responsibility to do everything in its power to ensure the health, safety and welfare of its construction workforce. In an industry with a reputation for disproportionately high levels of accident and work-related ill-health, the ODA reckoned it could expect around 1000 reportable accidents during the construction phase, based on HSE statistics, unless it developed a very clear strategy for a dramatic improvement on industry norms and practices.

As a new client with a multiplicity of challenges to deal with, the ODA established a peer group early in 2006, comprising leaders across the industry, who freely gave their time and expertise to the drafting of a standard that represented the best that the industry had done, up to that point, to achieve high performance. As a developer and procurement body ODA recognised that the key to performance is leadership. The executive directors of the ODA understood that the reasons for focussing on health and safety from the outset were three-fold:

- They accepted they had a moral obligation to seek to minimise harm to their workforce
- They understood that, as a client/employer ODA had duties under the Health & Safety at Work Act 1974 and subsidiary legislation, particularly the Construction (Design and Management) Regulations 1994.

- They recognised that good management involves managing risk-
  the relationship between the risks to the programme and their
  reputation, and the consequences of serious accidents or work
  related ill health were fully acknowledged.

With around 112 major construction and engineering contracts, there
was a danger of different standards and approaches being adopted by
the various designers and Tier 1 (principal) contractors who made up
the various project teams. Health and safety as a priority theme was
woven into everything the ODA and its delivery partner CLM did. The
base case for each project - the design brief and specification, the
methods of procurement and the wording of contracts and work
instructions – all reflected ODA requirements.

ODA recognised that good design can contribute to risk reduction, and
stimulated efforts to reduce risks through design review and
development. They created the role of CDM integrator who was
responsible for managing and co-ordinating the CDM co-ordinators
appointed for each project. This appointment of a 'super CDM co-
ordinator' was designed to ensure maximum value from their
interventions and provide a degree of consistency over a wide variety
of projects.

One example of the value of seeking a safer design was the roof of the
Velodrome venue. The initial concept design for the Velodrome roof
consisted of a steel truss structure which would have been erected at
its final level, utilising a crash deck. Although perfectly feasible, this
solution would have required substantial temporary works to enable
working at height, whilst restricting other works which had to be
carried out in the same locality. In addition, this solution introduced
long-term maintenance risks for the venue operator.

The project CDM co-ordinator, working with the design team, quickly
recognised the need to explore alternatives to the proposed steel truss
roof design and organised a design risk workshop to consider
alternative solutions which could reduce the risk to operatives both
during construction and operation of the venue. Following the
workshop, it was decided that a cable-net roof design would be both
safer and more cost-effective. The cable-net could be assembled at
ground level, fixed to node points and hydraulically jacked into its final
position. Temporary handrailing was designed to be fixed to the
leading edge of the roof before jacking operations began so that the

work which had to be completed at height could be done so at minimal risk to operatives. In addition to the contribution to safety, the revised roof design produced a saving of around 100ot of structural steelwork and consequential reduction in the size and depth of foundations.

It was a fundamental requirement of the ODA that any design solutions that reduced health and safety risks for construction workers and the end user should be shared with other London 2012 design teams. The Velodrome roof was one of many innovations that were shared across the Olympic site via design best practice forums and CDM co-ordination meetings.

Key learning points:-

1. The client recognised its moral and legal responsibilities and set out to establish an ethos that would influence the behaviour of all the organisations that would work on the delivery of the Olympic project.

2. Co-ordination of project information, both within individual projects and across the Olympic park was seen as vital to the successful delivery of London 2012. The appointment of a CDM integrator underlines the importance of the co-ordination role at the highest level of the project organisation.

3. When project teams are encouraged to think laterally and challenge the initial design concepts, major benefits can accrue both in financial and human terms.

THE CO-ORDINATION FUNCTION

If the project is notifiable, the client '*shall appoint a person (the CDM co-ordinator) to perform the duties specified in regulations 20 & 21 as soon as is practicable after initial design work or other preparations for construction work has begun.*'

Until such time as the client makes this appointment, they will be deemed to hold all the specified duties of the CDM co-ordinator (CDM-c) themselves.

The precise duties of a CDM-c will vary from project to project depending on the knowledge and experience of the client and the make-up of the project team. The appointment may be a stand-alone role or combined with another key function such as project manager or lead designer, and can be an individual or a company.

Unfortunately, in many cases the appointment is made much later than was intended in the regulations, where the design team has already done considerable detailed design work and the job of co-ordinating the design is much more difficult with many key decisions already 'finalised.' The problem has arisen partly out of a lack of understanding of the full scope of the co-ordination role or the benefits it can bring to the successful delivery of the project.

As many clients lack knowledge or experience of the construction process, the CDM-c is tasked to carry out various duties including:

- Notifying the HSE about the project
- Identifying and collecting pre-construction information
- Supplying relevant parts of this information –in a convenient form- to designers and contractors
- Advising the client on appointing competent designers and contractors
- Producing or updating a relevant, user-friendly safety file suitable for use after the construction phase.

The CDM-c also has to manage the information flow and promote communication and co-operation between members of the team. In reality this very simple requirement represents the biggest challenge, even to the most experienced and skilled CDM-c.

Unless the client is fully supportive of the need to fully assess the suitability of proposed design solutions, the whole process can be reduced to little more than a box-ticking exercise. As we have seen, there are times when the results of a design review can include major project cost and time savings as well as long-term reductions in maintenance costs. However, in some situations an additional cost may have to be sanctioned at the project stage in order to mitigate an unacceptable risk to construction or operational personnel. Designers and other project members are likely to be much more amenable to participating in a thorough assessment of their design if the client is actively engaged in the process.

Case Study 2: Getting it Right at Height

A large corporate client had commissioned a new 12-storey headquarters building in a city-centre location - a significant, landmark building valued at approximately £100m. The building was designed to be three-sided in plan with curved corners, the roof sloped from front to back in a series of steps and the office space was distributed round the perimeter of the building leaving the centre as an open space with a full-height atrium, allowing natural daylight to flood all areas of the offices.

The appointment of a professional CDM co-ordinator (CDM-c) had been made by the client at a very early stage in the development of the project. Although an outline building design had been produced, the client had not yet selected a site from three possible locations, and no detailed design work had been carried out.

In the early stages of the design development process the CDM-c organised a Hazard Identification Workshop (HIW). Unlike a traditional design team meeting, an HIW allows all members of the design team to partake in a brainstorming meeting chaired by the CDM-C; the purpose of such meetings is to identify areas of significant health and safety concern, both during the construction and operational phases, which can be logged and considered during the design development phase. Responsibilities are allocated to specific team members for further review with the aim of eliminating the hazard or reducing the risk prior to the construction phase, if at all possible.

One issue that was highlighted and discussed was the cleaning and minor maintenance of the external envelope and internal surfaces of the atrium. It was suggested that this issue needed further discussion and that a further workshop be set up primarily to review the options. Initially, a cradle system was considered the favourite means of access both to the external vertical facades and the underside of the atrium glazing.

As a major landmark project, the HSE had shown a great interest in the design stages of the scheme and it was decided to invite them to the second workshop. At this session the pros and cons of the proposed cradle scheme were discussed. The problems with this traditional solution were the stepped nature of the roof, the relatively 'sharp' corners of the three-sided building and the curved vertical facades that created a 'belly' shape, all of which limited the extent to which operatives could access the surfaces to be cleaned.

An alternative solution of rope access techniques was then proposed for the external envelope.

The relative merits of the two options were explored by the whole team, including the HSE representative. Although the cradle would offer a stable working platform, concerns were expressed about

- Areas difficult to access such as the corners and areas under the 'belly'
- The requirement to maintain the cradle equipment over the life of the building, when inspection and maintenance regimes can degrade.
- The difficulty of ensuring only trained and competent personnel operate and use the equipment over the life of the building
- The cost of constructing an elaborate support system for the cradle to operate from.

By comparison, the rope access option allowed cleaning of all areas of the facade, but only by skilled and experienced practitioners who would inspect and maintain their own equipment and would only require sufficient anchorage points to be designed and installed in the building's structure to allow access to all areas.

After careful deliberation, it was concluded that this was an option worth taking forward. Meetings were then held with specialist access providers and a solution was developed, with a rope access strategy being adopted at a saving of around £750,000.

By contrast, access to the underside of the atrium roof was deemed to be best served by a cradle system, due to the configuration of the stepped glazing.

Key learning points:-

1. Early appointment of the CDM-C allowed consideration of cleaning methodology to be developed before major design decisions had been taken. Although a key CDM issue, cleaning and associated access issues are often overlooked by project teams until the project is well advanced and the opportunity to select safer, and sometimes cheaper, solutions is restricted.

2. Initial hazard/risk assessment was carried out as a team activity, giving individual designers a clearer appreciation of which issues were to be given close attention during the detailed design phase.

3. Consideration of the Principles of Prevention would tend to suggest a cradle solution over rope access (giving collective protective measures priority over individual protective measures - Regulation 4, Management of Health & Safety at Work Regulations). However, a 'suitable and sufficient risk assessment'

requires a project team to consider all the factors relevant to that specific situation.

4. By involving specialist access providers in the process, the design team could feel more confident that their solution was not introducing greater risk than that being mitigated.

MANAGING THE DESIGN PROCESS

By now it should be clear that effective risk reduction requires a team approach. Many designers feel, quite rightly, that in isolation they are unable to determine the safest solution for a particular set of circumstances.

The design risk management process has two essential requirements:

1. The capacity to progressively review potential hazards as they become apparent during the planning and design phases of the project.

2. The ability to capture information relating to potential hazards and possible solutions as the team develops and grows, and a means for communicating the significant findings to other interested parties.

The role of the CDM co-ordinator is key to this process being managed from the inception of the project right through to the client's acceptance of the operational facility.

The size and nature of the project team will dictate the number of steps needed to fully assess the risks and how they should be addressed prior to construction commencing.

However, we would suggest that there are five stages that all project teams should progress through, before construction begins in earnest:-

1. Inception review
2. Design team briefing
3. Initial design development
4. Design risk review
5. Contractor appointment

1.   **Inception review**
     As soon as the client has appointed the CDM-co-ordinator an initial hazard identification workshop, with any lead designers already appointed, could be used to identify significant hazards likely to be encountered if the scheme progresses as envisaged.

This forum can provide a great opportunity for ensuring that everyone understands the importance of addressing and, where possible eliminating or reducing risk at an early stage.

For example, let's assume that the client is envisaging a development which involves significant structural steelwork. At this early stage it may be worth exploring the reasons for this preference and whether other options could offer a lower risk solution.

At this point a risk register or risk matrix could start to be developed.

2. **Design team briefing**
Irrespective of whether the design team has already been appointed, there is a requirement to assess the competence of those appointed by the client. This is best done by giving (prospective) members of the design team the information arising from the inception review and seeking their views on the likely risks and possible alternatives to the proposed solution

For example, issues identified might include
- Excessive working at height
- Lifting of large sections
- Corrosion protection requirements
- Access for deliveries
- Environmental considerations

Following the discussions:
a] The client and CDM-c will have an appreciation of the designers' attitude and capabilities towards designing out risk.
b] The designers will have a clear understanding of the design risk issues they should be mindful of when carrying out their design activities.

3. **Initial design development**
The designers can start to develop a solution taking into account technical and financial considerations as well as safety, health and environmental concerns, with the expectation that they will need to justify their proposals at the subsequent design risk review.

4. **Design risk review**
Having been briefed as to some of the main areas of concern at the previous meeting the designers will be in a better position to explain the reasons for their current preferred design at the subsequent design risk review. By this stage it is highly desirable to invite to the meeting

prospective contractors as well as operational and/or maintenance personnel who can provide a practical insight into the buildability and operability of the proposed design.

In addition to the contribution they can make, contractors can be assessed as to their competence based on the specific project requirements rather than the generic, organisation-level assessments that are currently the norm in the industry. A competent contractor would for example be able to advise on structural steelwork issues – whether it is better to fabricate larger sections which will reduce the amount of work at height but involve more complex lifting operations, or design for smaller elements that can be easily lifted but will requir more work at height. It is impossible to make a proper judgement of the most appropriate option without an appreciation of the contractor's proposed method of working, site conditions and access restrictions etc.

Likewise, operational and maintenance personnel can contribute to discussions about corrosion protection of the steelwork. Whereas the designer may be considering a protection system that involves lower cost but regular upkeep, operational staff can advise on the risks to personnel and impact on business activities, which may lead to a more expensive solution being adopted which will impact financially in the short term but will deliver long-term benefits to both the client and the workforce.

Designers should leave this meeting with a clear instruction from the client as to what is required, confident that the solution has been arrived at by a robust process and the requirements for design risk assessment have been fully met.

5.   **Contractor appointment**
If the contractor appointment follows their involvement in the design review process, clearly there will be a better understanding of the project requirements.

When appointing a contractor who has not been part of the process, consideration should be given as to how the information developed during the course of the design development process will be shared with the contractors' staff. It is always preferable to discuss these issues face to face rather than relying on written information or drawings. Whilst it is inevitably more time consuming, such meetings enable a two-way process of communication which will often generate benefits both to the client and the project team that far outweigh the extra time spent.

Case Study 3: A Tale of Two Power Stations

When a large energy services provider was appointed as Engineering, Procurement and Construction (EPC) contractor for a £2.5 million project at a nuclear power station, it drew on its previous experience as a contractor on a similar project at the station's sister site in another part of the UK, which had been completed the year before.

On both sites the project involved the modification of pipework and installation of new equipment to allow the temperature and pressure of steam condensate entering the reactor feed system to be controlled. Both stations, designed and constructed between the late 1970s and early 80s had previously operated with no means of controlling the boiler feed temperature, leading to accelerated pipework corrosion, process efficiency reduction, and the challenging of safety case operating limits. The scope of the project included the fabrication and erection of structural steelwork to support the rerouted pipework and new equipment on the roof of one of the main process buildings. As design information relating to the existing roof structure was not available, there was some concern regarding the distribution of superimposed loads resulting from the new installation.

A fully designed scaffold was required to provide both access for the installation crew and to enable rigging of lifting equipment for moving materials and equipment on the roof, which was inaccessible to craneage. On the previous project (P1) there had been minimal co-ordination of the temporary works design for the scaffolding (carried by a scaffolding contractor) with the design of the permanent installation (by the clients own technical team). As the available shutdown (outage) period was restricted to eight weeks the programme required the scaffolding structure to be designed and installed, in parallel with the design of the permanent works, prior to the start of the outage.

As a result of various design changes to the permanent works during the pre-construction phase, it became apparent shortly before the shutdown that there was a clash between some of the major scaffolding supports and elements of the structural steelwork. As a result the scaffolding had to be redesigned and modified at a very significant additional cost, and resulting in a three day delay to the programme.

It was recognised by the team from the second project (P2), which included some members who had worked on P1, that there was a need for better co-ordination, from the very start of the project. A project launch meeting was held nine months before construction was scheduled to begin, led jointly by the client's and the contractor's project managers and included the leads from the following disciplines:-

- Engineering
- Design
- Procurement
- Health & Safety
- Quality
- Commercial

The client began by explaining the purpose of the project and the benefits it would bring to the station and their business. The contractor's project manager then led the development of a preliminary risk register. With the lessons learned from the previous project in mind, a series of potential problems (risks) was identified. Each risk was allocated an owner, and discussions developed as to how each risk might be mitigated. Thereafter, regular project review meetings were convened, with the same membership, to review and update the register. After the first couple of review meetings it became apparent that for some of the identified risks, there was a lack of knowledge amongst those present, to enable proper evaluation and mitigation of the risk to be carried out. Subsequently, invitees included other client personnel in design, operational and maintenance roles as well as representatives from scaffolding and insulation contractors.

At one of these meetings, a discussion ensued regarding the removal of a section of condensate pipework to accommodate the erection of a section of support steelwork. An assumption had been made that, once the plant had shut down, the pipework could be cut and the steelwork erected immediately. One of those attending this meeting for the first time was one of the client's operational team leaders; she explained that once the plant was shut down, the system would need several days to cool down, before any pipework could be removed. She estimated the period to be at least five days and made it clear that no work would be permitted until permission was granted. As the risk was identified well in advance of construction work, one of the planned quarterly plant shutdowns was used to re-route the condensate pipe work removing the risk prior to construction commencement.

Key learning points:-

1. Unless all aspects of the project are co-ordinated effectively during the planning and design stages, the opportunities for expensive mistakes are almost unlimited.

2. Project co-ordination is a skilled function that requires careful consideration of people issues :-
   - Who is in the team?
   - What do they need to know?
   - Are we using the expertise in the team effectively?
   - How much time do we have available for planning and design?

3. Every project can provide lessons-learned for the benefit of future project teams.

THE RIGHT INFORMATION FOR THE RIGHT PEOPLE AT THE RIGHT TIME

Effective communication between the various parties involved with a project is the key to avoiding the pitfalls that can afflict any undertaking of this nature, whatever the size or scale of the job. Whether we are talking about Pre-construction information, the Construction Phase Health and Safety Plan or the Health and Safety File, there is a difference between '**producing documentation**' and '**communicating**'.

If the paperwork is not contributing to a two-way flow of information between the various members of the team it is reasonable to question its purpose – and its effectiveness.

Project teams should devote more time - not only at the inception of the project but throughout the delivery process - to asking each other: *'How we can ensure the right people get the right information?'*

One thing is for sure – **on its own the paperwork will achieve nothing.**

Build the team – then build the project.

Teamwork – not paperwork!

CONCLUSION

We hope that this book has given you an understanding of the true purpose of the CDM regulations, and an idea of what to do to improve the performance of project teams.

One thing we can be certain of, is that however much you agree with the concepts and processes discussed in the text, nothing will change unless action is taken.

And you are the person to take that action!

Each one of us can do what we can to move towards improving collaboration, communication and co-operation across the project teams of which we are part. And if we all do a little, we'll see a big change.

So good luck – and welcome to the team!